# GCSE ENGLISH LITERATURE for CCEA

SERIES EDITOR:
John Andrews

Len Quigg
Pauline Wylie

HODDER
EDUCATION
PART OF HACHETTE LIVRE UK

The Publishers would like to thank the following for permission to reproduce copyright material:
Photo credits: p.4 © Cooper Andrew/Corbis Sygma; p.11 © Two Arts/CD/The Kobal Collection; p.15 © Steve Skjold/ Alamy; p.20 © Pete Jones/Arena PAL/Topfoto; p.27 © Donald Cooper/Photostage; p.31 © Halas and Batchelor/BFI Stills; p.46 © SNAP/Rex Features; p.50 © Cooper Andrew/Corbis Sygma; p.56 © Hans Reinhard/Zefa/Corbis; p.62 (left) © Bettmann/Corbis; (middle) © Bettman/Corbis; (right) © Hulton-Deutsch Collection/Corbis; p.70 © Werner Forman/Corbis; p.71 © Renee Morris/Alamy.

Every effort has been made to trace all copyright holders, but if any have been inadvertently overlooked the Publishers will be pleased to make the necessary arrangements at the first opportunity.



Orders: please contact Bookpoint Ltd, 130 Milton Park, Abingdon, Oxon OX14 4SB. Telephone: (44) 01235 827720. Fax: (44) 01235 400454. Lines are open 9.00 - 5.00, Monday to Saturday, with a 24-hour message answering service. Visit our website at www.hoddereducation.co.uk


First published in 2007 by
Hodder Education, part of Hachette Livre UK
338 Euston Road
London NW1 3BH

Impression number 10 9 8 7 6 5 4 3 2
Year 2011 2010 2009 2008



Cover photo © Richard Cummins/Corbis
Typeset in ITC Legacy Sans Book 12pt by DC Graphic Design Limited, Swanley, Kent.
Printed in Great Britain by CPI Antony Rowe

A catalogue record for this title is available from the British Library.

ISBN: 978 0340 92935 3

# CONTENTS





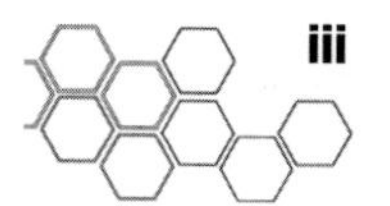

# Introduction

## The purpose of the book

Let's begin by making clear what this text will *not* do! It will not provide you with an analysis of the set books you are studying for this examination, nor will it ensure that you will have the close textual knowledge you require to be able to answer the particular questions that come up in your exam. So, what *is* its purpose, you ask? Well that is simple to state (even if it is, in reality, somewhat more difficult to execute). We aim to help you take your acquired knowledge and understanding and apply these to the examination questions, so that you maximise your performance when it comes to those three essay questions that await you in May/June.

It is essential that you are aware of the different demands made by each of the questions and that you understand the appropriate styles of response. To be successful, you will have worked within rigorous timescales; unpacked questions; planned relevant answers; displayed breadth and depth of knowledge; analysed themes and drawn relevant material together; recognised the required degree of detail; and developed three fluent, ordered and coherent pieces of writing. These are the skills that form the focus of this book.

The ability to generate an essay that effectively delivers knowledge and critical understanding is too often forgotten about in the hustle and bustle of revision. It is all too easy to under-perform despite having a clear appreciation of the novel, play and poetry studied.

It is critical that you know exactly how much of each 50-minute essay writing slot will be given over to the business of reading, analysing and planning your answer. In the time remaining, how much can you physically write? This one very basic factor will control the level of detail that can be included in your essay. Also, remember that the three essays must be written fluently and coherently.

Knowing the answers to these basic questions is part of being properly organised. It is the business of every thoroughly prepared student to understand the challenges ahead and how they can be successfully met. A proper performance in the GCSE English Literature examination is not down to good luck - it is a matter of thorough and sensible preparation.

This book will present a detailed discussion of the business of writing answers and will also analyse all the available question types. Exemplar essays have been included; these are annotated in order to highlight the strengths and weaknesses of the answers. Sample questions and checklists are also provided, so you can practise and assess your essay writing.

Recognising the demands of the examination and understanding how these demands can be met, puts you in control. *That* is the purpose of this book.

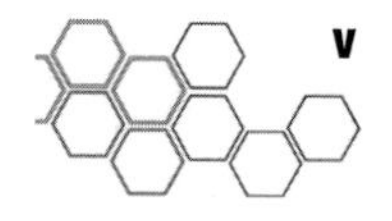

## How the book is organised

The first chapters deal with the basics of the examination. These are outlined in order to ensure that candidates (and concerned parents) understand the rationale that underpins the GCSE English Literature Specification. The complete specification for the examination can be found on CCEA's website at ccea.org.uk

The core of the book - Chapters 3, 4 and 5 - mirrors the examination, as the three genres are presented here in the same order that they appear in the exam paper.

Each of these chapters will provide useful opportunities for practice, presenting a range of questions that are similar in style and content to those that will be faced in the actual examination.

## Basic information about CCEA's GCSE English Literature examination

| | **Two possible tiers of entry** | **Available grades** |
|---|---|---|
| **GCSE English Literature** | Foundation | C–G |
| | Higher | A*–D (E is also awarded) |

| | **Time allocation and elements within the exam** |
|---|---|
| **Examination:** one paper<br>70% of overall mark<br>2½ hours | **Section A:** 50 minutes<br>**Drama:** a choice of two questions will be offered on each of the prescribed texts. |
| | **Section B:** 50 minutes<br>**Prose:** a choice of two questions will be offered on each of the prescribed texts. |
| | **Section C:** 50 minutes<br>**Poetry:** a choice of two questions will be offered on each of the anthologies. |

| | **Three assignments** |
|---|---|
| **Coursework**<br>30% of overall mark<br>Internally assessed | **Assignment A**<br>Essay response to poetry from our own and other cultures published after 1914. |
| | **Assignment B**<br>Essay response to a Shakespeare play. |
| | **Assignment C**<br>Essay response to prose written before 1914. |

# Chapter 1: Assessment Objectives and their role

We begin by looking at the subject of assessment and it should be encouraging to note the following comment from the latest Mark Scheme: *Every effort should be made to assess the work of the candidate positively.* In other words, a positive form of marking is being employed – you will be credited for what you have achieved, rather than having marks deducted for mistakes and omissions!

To be honest, to spend time studying the finer points of Assessment Objectives is never going to be inspiring, but there are some important issues within these that will make reading this chapter worthwhile – even if you only read it once!

## What are Assessment Objectives?

They are the skills and abilities that are central to the development of an appreciation for English Literature. It is your ability to display the knowledge and skills that lies at the heart of these objectives that will be tested. For this reason alone, they merit a little of your attention.

### A summary of the Assessment Objectives (AO 1, 2, 3 and 4)

**AO 1** Respond critically, sensitively and in detail to texts, using evidence from texts appropriately to develop a point of view.

**AO 2** Understand how language, structure and form contribute to meaning.

**AO 3** Explore relationships and comparisons between texts, selecting and evaluating material.

**AO 4** Relate texts to their social, historical and cultural background (this is only tested in Coursework in Assignments B and C).

It is easier to understand the three exam-tested Assessment Objectives if they are seen as a range of abilities that you have to develop:

## AO 1

- demonstrating understanding, insight and knowledge of the text
- inferring, deducing and supporting perspectives and interpretations with relevant references to the text
- presenting personal preferences and opinions that are supported and convincing.

## AO 2

- reflecting upon different views and interpretations of the text
- commenting on how form and structure are employed by the writer for effect
- demonstrating an awareness of the main characteristics of a writer's style and the effect of his/her use of language and stylistic devices
- understanding how mood, atmosphere and tone are controlled and used.

## AO 3

- recognising and exploring similarities and differences between texts in terms of:
  - theme, character and tone
  - language structure and form.

These lists seem daunting and very demanding! Don't be put off – to be aware of what is being assessed means that you can begin to grasp what is required of you!

The CCEA English Literature examination requires you to have made an in-depth study of one drama text, one prose text and one poetry anthology. The first two Assessment Objectives are clearly relevant to drama, prose and poetry. Asking you to look at two or more poems is, however, the only way to test the third Assessment Objective, with its emphasis on comparison. This is one of the important points to pick up here – only the poetry question will test **all three** of the Assessment Objectives. This has significance for your approach to this particular question, and the implications of this will be developed later.

# How the Assessment Objectives become part of the assessment process

Each section of the exam is testing the Assessment Objectives as outlined below:

| Section | AOs |
|---|---|
| Section A: Drama | AO 1 and 2 |
| Section B: Prose | AO 1 and 2 |
| Section C: Poetry | AO 1, 2 and 3 |

The Mark Scheme consists of three elements:

1 The significant skills from the Assessment Objectives that relate to the specific section of the exam are selected. These underpin the next two elements of the Mark Scheme.

2 A series of question-specific points are listed. These are the points that the examiner believes might be expected to form the basis of a typical answer. (You'll see lots of these lists in Chapter 6.)

3 An Assessment Matrix consists of a series of stepped Mark Band Descriptors. These Mark Bands describe progressively improving levels of performance. The actual score that is awarded is arrived at by selecting the Mark Band that most appropriately describes the qualities of the answer you've presented.

A brief glance at the Assessment Matrix below – for Higher Tier, Section C: Poetry 2005 – shows the inclusion of AO 3.

| **Assessment Objective** | **Band 1 Marks 0–5** | **Band 2 Marks 6–15** | **Band 3 Marks 16–25** |
|---|---|---|---|
| **AO 1**<br>**Argument** (developing a point of view on the question) | Some writing about text or task. | Simple, straightforward or limited response.<br>Attempt to focus on the question.<br>Assertion, basic conclusion, narrative or description. | Begins to develop a response. / Fairly developed response.<br>Begins to focus on question. / Some focus on question.<br>Some arguments. |
| **AO 2**<br>**Form and Language** | Simplistic comments about characters, setting and events.<br>Little or no awareness of setting, form or prose techniques. | Some awareness of significance of characters, setting and events.<br>Some awareness of structure, form or prose techniques.<br>Occasional reference to the writer's words. | Comments on characters, setting and events.<br>Comments on structure, form or techniques.<br>Some understanding of the writer's use of language. |
| **AO 3**<br>**Comparison and Contrast** | Poems considered in isolation. | Simple connections made between poems. | Attempt to explore obvious comparisons and contrasts between poems. |

This example should make it clear why the whole business of Assessment Objectives has been given such a prominent position – they lie at the heart of each of the Assessment Matrixes.

Now we've established the nature of the links between the Assessment Objectives and their role in the examining process, it is time to begin analysing the demands of the questions and the skills you require to deal with them successfully!

# Chapter 2: Effective essay writing

Writing competent essays is not a product of luck. At GCSE level, it is a matter of applying knowledge in a relevant and organised manner.

## Qualities and characteristics of an effective essay answer

It is essential that we are aware of the qualities and characteristics of an effective essay answer – after all, 70 per cent of the overall mark allocation is given to the three essays you will write in the exam! The ability to produce three competent essays in two and a half hours is one of the major keys to success, so it's important that we have a sound grasp of the components that go together to make an 'efficient' essay.

### Activity 2.1

Individually, in pairs or small groups, take 10–15 minutes to make a list of the important qualities and features that would be essential in the development of a competent essay. *See Checklists on page 73.*

Below is a question taken from a Literature Paper. It is followed by a competent response. The answer is annotated in order to highlight how this essay matches the indicators set out in our checklist. When seen in use, these qualities are not quite so threatening. (Don't worry if this is not based on one of your set texts, as the focus is on the qualities of the essay not its content.)

**Steinbeck: *Of Mice and Men***

**This question is about power.**

Show that Steinbeck presents three characters who have differing kinds of power. Which kind of power do you think is the most destructive? Give reasons for your opinions.

In your answer you should consider:

- George
- Lennie
- Curley.

*George, Lennie and Curley all have large amounts of power through the entire novel but they have different kinds.*

*George 'A small man, dark of face with dark eyes and sharp features' has power over Lennie, he is a father figure to him, we see this at the very beginning when George takes the mouse from Lennie. Lennie is very forgetful and George is constantly reminding him of where they are going and what they are doing 'So ya' forgot that awready'. George minds his work slip for him as he knows that it is more than likely that Lennie will lose it. Lennie is treated as a child by George and Lennie in turn treats George like a father figure.*

*Lennie 'A huge man, with pale eyes and sloping shoulders, he dragged his feet a little when he walked, the way a bear drags its paws' on the other hand Lennie has physical strength, he often kills mice by stroking them to hard. He is unaware of this strength and cannot control it. We next see this strength when Curley starts to fight with him 'Come on ... No son-of-a-bitch gonna laugh at me ... I'll show ya whos yella'. Lennie does not want to fight with Curley but in the end he crushes his hand. He does this after George encourages him to fight back 'Get 'im Lennie ... I said get 'im' Lennie grabs Curley's hand but does not know when to let go, he does not realise the damage he is doing 'I didn't want to hurt 'im'. Lennie uses this uncontrolable physical strength again in the killing of the puppy and Curley's wife. He loves to stroke soft things and when Slim gives him the puppy he accidently kills it by stroking it to hard. A similar incident happened with Curley's wife, she is a very flirtatious women and when she invites him to touch her soft hair he can not resist 'it is so soft ... right around there ... feel right around there its so soft, Lennie feels her hair but gets to rough and she panics, this is similar to the incident which happened in Weed. '"Don't you go yellin" Lennie shook her and her body flopped like a fish ... She was still for Lennie had broken her neck.'*

*Curley has power over the men on the ranch because 'His old mans the boss'. Curley is 'A small man, dark face, dark eyes and tightly curled hair'. Although he has all the power he is a weak and insecure man, this may be due to the fact that he is disliked by everyone on the ranch including his wife. He is suspicious of his wife and the other men on the ranch as he believes she may be having an affair with one of them, he is particularly suspicious of Slim 'Is weary of Slim and Slim in turn is not afraid of him.'*

*It is my opinion that Lennie's power is the most destructive, although it is unintentional, his power and strength has had the worst consequences. His power led him to the killing of animals, the mice and the puppy, the killing of another being, Curley's wife, and finally it has led to the killing of himself.*

A straightforward introduction that re-states the question drawing attention to the key issue – 'kinds of power'.

An effective combination of quotation, evidence and concluding analysis develop the sense of a candidate tackling the first element of the task in a relevant manner.

You will note that the same basic arrangement has been used to consider this character as was used for the first. This formula is repeated again when the writer goes on to deal with the final character mentioned in the question.

This time there is greater depth to the analysis with a wide range of appropriate examples presented.

Perhaps the final reference here is too detailed. The temptation to include yet another quote means that the emphasis here is very much on relating incident and fails to relate back to the central focus – 'kinds of power'.

The opening sentence clearly keeps the answer on task. Following the now-familiar opening piece of description, the third sentence offers relevant analysis.

Again focused on task, this candidate finishes off by dealing with the final element of the question.

There is a real attempt to conclude the essay with a strong summative remark.

The commentary should make it clear how this essay meets the 'competent essay' criteria.

The writer has:

✓ focused on the question throughout

✓ clearly organised the response, working through all the elements in the question

✓ been selective, presenting relevant examples appropriately supported by quotations to examine the issue of power

✓ shown both breadth and depth of knowledge (looked at some incidents in detail and on other occasions made general reference to further relevant incidents)

✓ produced an answer that is balanced in terms of analysis and exemplification

✓ generally expressed the answer succinctly and effectively.

It would also be fair to say that this response is not perfect (remember, it was written under exam conditions – a fact that examiners recognise). It was not selected for excellence; the reason for including it was to demonstrate the significant elements of a competent answer in action, and how they can be successfully combined!

## Activity 2.2

If you are familiar with this text, individually or in groups, consider:

- What other material should or could have been included?
- Which pieces of this response could be pruned to make way for your proposed additions?
  *See Checklists on page 73.*

## Activity 2.3

Imagine you are in the exam and have just completed writing this response. You have *5 minutes* left to make minor modifications and corrections before moving on to the next question. Make a list of the alterations you would make in that time.
*See Checklists on page 73.*

## Appropriate tone, style, writing stance, degree of personal involvement

A generally **formal tone** is most appropriate. Imagine you are writing for a teacher you don't know – this in all probability will be your audience! Here are a couple of examples that should give a sense of the required approach:

Descriptive language such as 'ripeness to the core' gives the reader a vivid picture as to how Keats feels about Autumn.

When Atticus takes on Tom Robinson's case, he demonstrates bravery and defiance as well as self-confidence and composure.

Aim for an **uncomplicated style**. After all, you will be writing under the pressure of limited time; long, complex sentences tend to be time-consuming to write and are likely to contain a higher error count. Avoid slang and imprecise vocabulary, and try to keep your writing concise, straightforward and fluent, as in this example:

The Stage Manager in this play has the role of filling in gaps in the plot that are not explained through dialogue.

An **impersonal writing stance** is most appropriate in this situation:

Steinbeck captures his reader's attention as the inevitable tragedy unfolds …

or

The audience is caught up by the frenzy of the dancing sisters as one by one they give themselves up to …

Avoid the following approach, in which the over-personal style of the writing really gets in the way of what the individual is trying to say:

You think that you are there because the poet makes you feel …

What of **your opinion**? If the question asks for it, then you should not be afraid to present it. By all means be lively and engaging. Just because the nature of the writing is formal, it doesn't mean it has to be boring as well! Strongly held, relevantly supported and fluently expressed views will score highly:

I feel more sympathy for Hood, as in 'A Parental Ode', his patience is relentlessly tried by his small son. In 'Remember', it is slightly more difficult to feel sorry for the writer as …

# Organising your time

This section suggests how you should split your allotted 50 minutes for each essay into selection, planning, writing, rereading and correcting time.

## Time management

'I hadn't time to finish!' or 'They didn't give me enough time!' are simply different forms of an excuse that uncomfortably masks a series of possible scenarios. And you do not want to be a part of any of the following:

*I lacked the organisational skills I should have had in order to finish the exam – in other words, I didn't prepare properly.*

or

*I didn't have the self-discipline to manage my time properly.*

or

*I am not prepared to face up to reality and would rather blame someone else, in this case the examiners, for my own shortcomings!*

The key to maximising your performance - producing your best possible response - will revolve around your ability to:

- ✓ manage your time effectively
- ✓ sustain a sensible, methodical approach.

As a candidate in this type of exam, you will **always** score more highly if you produce three solid answers than you will if you come up with two good answers and a third one half a page long that concludes in note form (or with a heartfelt plea to your marker because you've run out of time).

Having established the importance of these three, 50-minute slots, what do you need to do, organisationally, to produce competent responses?

The following four steps show you how to work your way effectively through the process of producing these 50-minute essays.

### Reading and selecting (5 minutes)

It is ironic that the most significant advice is something you will have heard a thousand times before: R-T-Q ⟶ READ THE QUESTION!

At some time or another, we have all experienced the following scenario. You are in the exam room in a state of nervous tension, itching to begin. So what happens? As a direct result of your natural urge to be getting on with it, you glance over the questions, make your choice and jump straight in - only to discover halfway through your answer that you didn't fully grasp what was required and, as a result, you've included a considerable amount of irrelevant material.

The accompanying sinking feeling that attacks the pit of the stomach is not an experience anyone would want to revisit in June, so beware the urge to get off to a quick start!

The key words in questions will already be in bold. You can highlight or circle them again if it helps you to focus on the main issues and requirements. Avoid the temptation to make a snap judgement – read both questions, (a) and (b), carefully. Weigh up which offers you the better chance to demonstrate your knowledge and understanding. Once you've sorted out the answer to that, you've made your first decision and you're already on to stage two.

## Planning your answer (no less than 10 minutes)

Time spent thinking and planning is time well spent. Unless you take a few minutes to gather and organise your ideas, you will not be in a position to produce your best answer. If you look back at the checklist of criteria that are to be found in a competent essay (see page 6), you will realise that planning facilitates every one of these. To get your essay organised, you must make a plan!

A plan brings logic to your writing, creating a sense that there is a coherent thread running through your answer. It also offers the considerable benefit that you are not in that complicated situation where you have to consider *how* you are expressing yourself, while also trying to think about *what* is coming next!

Plan using an approach that suits you. This could involve: some form of brainstorming/annotating of your question paper, which you sort into some appropriate order; or you could create a spider diagram or mind map in your answer booklet. Whatever you do – MAKE A PLAN!

Don't be tempted to write out complete sentences – work with key words and phrases, as you don't have time for anything more detailed!

### Activity 2.4

Take ten minutes to produce your own style of plan for the following *Anthology One* poetry question.

**Question 12(a)**

**This question is about the seasons.**

Look again at 'To Autumn' by John Keats, and at **either** 'Shall I Compare Thee to a Summer's Day?' by William Shakespeare **or** 'The Darkling Thrush' by Thomas Hardy.

From the way these two poems about the seasons are written, show how the poems are alike and how they are different, and explain which of the two poems you prefer.

In your answer, you should consider:

- what each poet has written about
- what you learn about the thoughts and feelings expressed in each poem
- anything else you think is relevant.

## Writing the essay (30 minutes of actual writing)

Long before you ever reach the examination-room door, it is fundamental to your preparation that you understand how much you can *sensibly and accurately* write in 30 minutes. Notice that 'sensibly and accurately' is in italics. It is better to write a little less and express yourself coherently and relatively accurately than to write more but in an uncontrolled and inaccurate manner.

Knowing how much you can write in this time span is very important. You need to assess roughly how much detail you can afford to go into for each of the paragraphs you have come up with in your plan. For instance, if you have four main points/paragraphs to write and two and a half sides is the limit of your writing in 30 minutes, it's easy to recognise that you can write about half a page for each point, leaving you with a half-page (combined) for your introduction and conclusion. This is basic preparation and common sense, but it's all part of being 'exam-ready'.

Once you have planned your essay, the task of concentrating on expressing yourself accurately and concisely becomes much easier. This is still a creative and demanding process, with the most difficult elements of an essay being the introduction and the conclusion. These two paragraphs set the tone for what is to come, and draw the piece to what you hope will be a fitting close.

Make sure you maintain your focus on the question. Lead the examiner through the points you are making by using clear paragraph links and sensible sentence structuring. Remember to aim for that relatively uncomplicated style. That does not mean, however, that you shouldn't try to vary sentence length for effect or make use of rhetorical devices to keep your reader interested.

As you are writing the essay, continue to focus your writing on the question's central issue - don't be afraid to relate your ideas back to the main theme as you develop your essay, as this shows the examiner you are 'on task'. Other relevant points are likely to spring to mind while you are writing your answer; do make use of these while attempting (as far as possible) to incorporate them into your overall plan.

Try to finish strongly or thoughtfully. Don't end on a rather lame comment or by repeating the introduction.

### Activity 2.5

In the sample answer on page 5, you will find an example of a rather ordinary introduction. Take 2 or 3 minutes to see if you can produce a more effective opening to the essay.

### Activity 2.6

Write your own introductory and concluding paragraphs for the question in Activity 2.4. Share these with either your group or your classmates.

## Rereading and revising (last 5 minutes)

In this final element of the essay-writing process you need to view your writing from a different angle. The first 45 minutes have been spent in a creative process – making your answer. During the last 5 minutes, you have to stand back and objectively reassess your response. Imagine someone else has written this piece, and it is your task – in 5 minutes – to find the mistakes and glitches and sort them out. Here are the sorts of things you are looking for:

- words that have been left out
- inappropriate word choices that can be improved upon
- overly long sentences
- inappropriate repetition of either words or sentence openings
- awkward phrases that could be expressed more fluently.

This is every bit as intense as the creative process that has gone before. Don't delude yourself: there will be minor errors and odd sentences that have 'gone astray', so make sure you sort out as many of these as possible.

Remember: every mistake you correct is one fewer for your examiner to spot; you are literally saving yourself marks as you make these final revisions!

### Activity 2.7

Here is an excerpt from an exam response. It is the introduction to a question on the novel *How Many Miles to Babylon?* The writer is trying to explain how Alexander changes during the course of the novel.

Rewrite it so that it is expressed accurately and fluently.

Alexander is described as being a sensitively natured boy and as the novel progresses, he matures and gets tougher, but he also retains a sensitive side to him. In the novel Alexander shows a caring attitude to others in the novel.

*See Checklists on page 73.*

### Activity 2.8

This is one paragraph from an essay on William Golding's *Lord of the Flies*. The writer is analysing the differences between the character called Piggy and the other boys with whom he shares the island.

Improve this section by making changes to make it read more fluently.

Some things that Piggy says suggests that he is different to the other boys. He says 'I've had asthma ever since I was wee' suggesting that his health has also made him an outsider but the main point to make about this is that he says it with pride. This automatically makes him feel he is better than others in some ways, if not physically. He boasts 'My Aunty owns a sweet shop' suggesting that he has to try and make himself seem better and more interesting in order to fit in.

*See Checklists on page 74.*

## 'Dos and don'ts'

In this final section, we present a summary of the pitfalls to avoid, as well as a list of the positive steps to build into your essay-writing strategy. Pay careful attention to them. Ignore them at your peril!

### Don't:

- ✗ begin without thinking and planning
- ✗ tell the story
- ✗ lose focus on the question
- ✗ use long quotations in an 'open-book' exam
- ✗ include a quotation just because you know it!
- ✗ ignore the allocated time
- ✗ make generalised and unsupported statements.

### Do:

- ✓ carefully consider the requirements of the question
- ✓ pick out and highlight the key words
- ✓ plan your response
- ✓ make use of any prompts in the question
- ✓ lead the examiner through your answer
- ✓ balance the different elements within the question
- ✓ explain the significance of incidents in relation to the question
- ✓ express yourself concisely and fluently
- ✓ avoid complicated sentence constructions
- ✓ stick to your time limits.

# Chapter 3: The drama section

## The nature of drama

It seems an obvious statement to make, but plays are written and designed to be seen as pieces of live drama! To really appreciate a play, nothing beats the experience of being in a theatre, watching and listening as the action and dialogue unfold before your eyes. Skilful actors supported by theatrical effects such as lighting, sound and costuming bring a play to life.

When you are reading and studying drama, always try to imagine how what you are studying would appear on a stage. If the opportunity arises, it is important to go and see a performance of the play you are studying. It will enhance your grasp of the play and reinforce the dramatic elements that combine to make well-performed drama such a powerful medium.

## The components of the playwright's craft

To write a good play, a playwright must create and combine various components in order to hold an audience's attention. Among these main 'ingredients' will be:

- a gripping storyline or plot
- a story that develops and then unfolds
- credible 'flesh and blood' characters
- problems/conflicts or issues that have to be resolved
- an outcome – it may be a happy one, or conversely it can end tragically.

In this chapter, we will first focus our attentions on these constituent parts. We will consider how to cope most effectively with the demands of the questions to be faced in the Drama section of the GCSE examination.

## The development of plot and structure

These are closely linked. Here are a couple of definitions of these two important elements:

- **plot:** how the storyline develops – with all its twists, turns and unexpected incidents
- **structure:** how a playwright develops and divides the storyline into different segments.

### Plot

Clearly, one of the most basic requirements is that you have a sound grasp of the plot. This section of the examination is 'plain text', so you don't want to be wasting time searching for the additional textual references or quotes you want to include as you move your answer beyond the given extract. If, before your mock examination, you are still asking yourself questions such as 'Did that happen before or after ...?' you simply don't know your text well enough!

Activity 3.1 is designed to help familiarise you with the events of the play you are studying.

**Activity 3.1**

In groups:

1 Select the key moments in the play you are studying.
2 Pick a quotation to represent each of these key moments.
3 List them in order.
4 Pass your list of quotations to another group, who must work out what key events have been selected and put those key events in sequence.

*Note:* An extension task would involve a spokesperson from each group having to justify the choices made by their group to the rest of the class. They could explain why these quotations aptly illustrate the most significant events in the action.

## Structure

As has already been said, plot and structure are closely connected. Plays are often structured into several **acts**, made up from a number of **scenes**, each of which moves the story forward or (as is sometimes the case) flashes back to the past.

Structure is also linked to:

- Changes in **mood** or **atmosphere**. This keeps the audience interested and helps direct them as to how to react to the characters and action. In two-act plays there is often a distinct change in mood, with the first act being light-hearted with the mood darkening in the second act as the story builds up to its dramatic **climax** (the play's most critical and dramatic moment).
- The **pace** or speed at which the action unfolds. A playwright will vary the speed at which things happen, in order to create particular effects such as an increase in tension or a sense of excitement. Often events happen in quick succession or there is a series of crises as the action builds up towards the climax of the performance.
- The **time sequence**. A common dramatic device is the use of **flashbacks**. The dramatic purpose of letting an audience glimpse the past in this way is to provide more insight into what motivates characters, therefore giving a much deeper understanding of their behaviour. Some plays can be quite complex with the use of flashbacks and time shifts.

Activity 3.2 is intended to help you appreciate how the playwright has structured your play in terms of mood, pace and timing in order to maximise the impact for an audience.

**Activity 3.2**

You have already identified the key moments in your play in Activity 3.1.
The next step is to use the grid on page 15 as a guide. Chart how these key events connect to the changes in mood, pace and time throughout the drama.
*Note:* This is only a suggested format. Instead, you may wish to think of these issues in terms of how your play is divided up into acts and scenes.

| Key/significant moments | Mood and atmosphere | Pace of action | Time sequence |
| --- | --- | --- | --- |
| The opening sequence | | | |
| First key moment | | | |
| Second key moment | | | |
| Next key moment (and so on, as required ...) | | | |
| Climax | | | |
| How the play concludes | | | |

## How dramatists present character

We learn about the characters in a play mainly through the dialogue and action, but some playwrights also give detailed descriptions and background information about particular characters.

You need to 'get to know' the characters in your text really well and come to an understanding of what motivates them to act as they do. Activities 3.3 and 3.4 are designed to help you achieve this.

### Activity 3.3

Working together in groups, use the spider diagram on page 16 as a way of building up detailed information on each character in the play.

This could be done in the form of posters for classroom display. Each group could take on responsibility for a particular character and report their findings to the rest of the class.

### Activity 3.4

Hot-seating is an effective way of considering a character.

Decide which character is to be the focus.
In groups, take 10 minutes to agree on four constructive questions to ask this character. Pupils can take turns to role-play the character (take the 'hot seat') and answer the prepared questions.

Another variation is to imagine that it is ten years after the events in the play. Someone, in character, takes the 'hot seat' and reminisces about what happened, reflecting on any consequences.

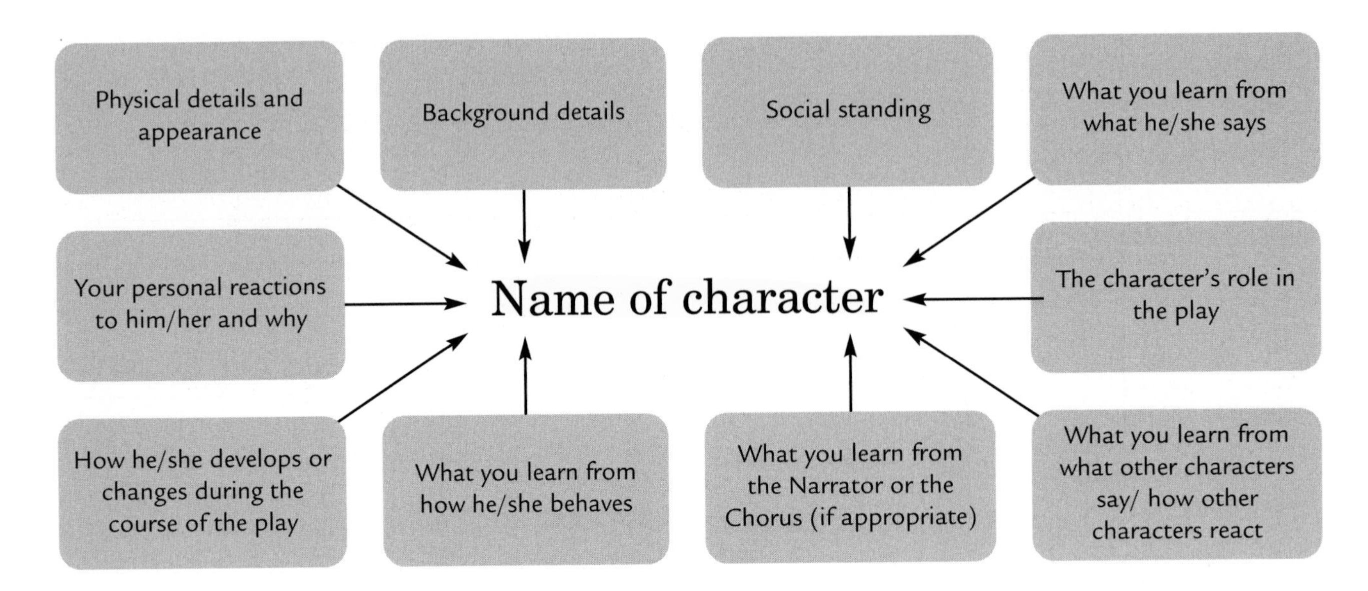


The (a) question in the Drama section of your examination will focus on analysing **how** a dramatist **presents** one or more of his/her characters. How the writer sets about presenting or **revealing** his/her characters to the audience is called **characterisation.** This is also how the writer **influences our feelings** towards characters and the situations they are in. As a result, we may empathise with one character while hoping another will get his/her come-uppance!

## Stage directions and other theatrical devices

As stated earlier, dialogue and actions play a crucial part in a play in terms of how a character is depicted. However, there are also a number of significant, theatrical devices that a playwright can employ in the delivery of his/her drama. The most influential of these is the use of **stage directions**.

The extent and degree of precision with which these are used varies. During your coursework study of Shakespearean drama, you will probably have noticed that his use of stage directions was extremely basic – Shakespeare rarely offered more assistance than to mark entrances and exits. This is why it is possible to offer so many varied interpretations of his plays. Modern dramatists tend to be more supportive and expansive in their use of stage directions and this is helpful in enabling all involved in a production to fulfil the writer's dramatic intentions.

Stage directions are the writer's means of orchestrating his/her drama, providing:

- background information
- details regarding physical appearance/personal facts
- directions on how actors should deliver particular lines/react
- instructions regarding movement, lighting or sound effects.

There are other **dramatic techniques** that the playwright puts to good use – the set, soliloquies/asides; a chorus or narrator to directly address the audience; Friel even uses the dramatic conceit of an imaginary boy in *Dancing at Lughnasa*.

Activity 3.5.1 gives the opportunity for essential practice in the skill of analysing **how** these dramatic devices have been integrated into the play you are studying.

## Activity 3.5.1

This is a group work exercise. The teacher will allocate each a different key scene/extract and character.

It is the task of each group to use the checklist headings on this page and page 18 – as appropriate – to answer the question:

**'How does the writer present the character to the audience in this extract?'**

*Note:* This task can then be widened to instruct groups to consider what they learn from:

- elsewhere in Act 1
- elsewhere in the play.

(These bullet points are typical instructions in the examination questions. They are far too frequently overlooked.)

## Activity 3.5.2

The teacher will divide up the class into groups and the play into the same number of segments. Each group will be assigned a portion of the play, so that when the task is completed, the whole class will have charted how a particular character is presented **throughout** the play.

The task of each group is to use the checklist headings on this page and page 18 – as appropriate – to answer the following question:

**'How does the writer present the character to the audience in your section of the play?'**

| For use with **Activities 3.5.1** and **3.5.2** **Scene/Character:** | | |
|---|---|---|
| **First impressions:**<br>How the character is introduced to the audience if this is his/her first appearance on stage | | |
| **The use of stage directions:**<br>• background information<br>• details regarding physical appearance/personal facts<br>• instructions on how actors should deliver particular lines<br>• instructions regarding movement, lighting or sound effects | | |
| **The use of dialogue:**<br>• what they say to others<br>• how others reply to them<br>• voice tones, e.g. anger, concern, sarcasm<br>• use of dialect | | |
| **The use of asides or monologues** | | |
| **What a Narrator or Chorus says about the characters** | | |

*Continued*

<table>
<tr><td colspan="3">For use with Activities 3.5.1 and 3.5.2 Scene/Character:</td></tr>
<tr><td>The use of actions:<br>• what he/she does to others<br>• how others behave/react in response<br>• any unexpected actions/responses<br>• how the character enters and exits the stage<br>• the pace of the action</td><td></td><td></td></tr>
<tr><td>The use of language/particular words and phrases:<br>• how this reflects the character's mood and that of others<br>• how personality is revealed through the character's choice of language<br>• the use of humour<br>• the use of colloquial speech/formal speech</td><td></td><td></td></tr>
<tr><td>The use of setting:<br>• the importance of location to the character<br>• the relevance of descriptions of place included in the stage directions<br>• how the historical setting helps us understand the character<br>• the significance of social setting to the character<br>• the use of flashbacks to another time/place<br>• how the general mood/atmosphere affects how we feel towards the character</td><td></td><td></td></tr>
</table>

## Themes in drama and their links to character

Question (b) in the Drama section of your examination will focus on analysing **how** a dramatist **presents** a theme.

**Themes** are the **issues and ideas** which a playwright highlights and explores in a play, for example superstition, family life or social position. Through watching the action unfold, an audience is influenced and led to reflect upon such issues. This is what the playwright **intends** to happen. For example, if a character is being portrayed in an unsympathetic light it is likely that, as well as offering his/her character for an audience to judge, the playwright may additionally be conveying his/her own negative views about a particular issue.

The previous section asked you to consider how characters are presented in your play. This was important to do, as themes also become clear when you study how the characters and action are being presented to the audience.

It is crucial, therefore, that you understand the **connections** between **themes** and **how the playwright presents his/her characters**. It is by looking at **how** the characters are presented that the themes are explored and the main messages revealed to the audience.

The activities in this section should help you become aware of and establish the links relevant to your text.

## Activity 3.6

1 With your teacher's help, in groups or individually, make a list of the themes that relate to your play.

2 Using the themes from your list as headings, decide which of them are relevant to each of the characters in your text. (It is very likely that you discover that individual characters will be linked to more than one theme!)

3 Now categorise the characters according to:

- those you like/don't like
- those who you feel sorry for/ those you don't
- their gender
- their age
- whether they are rich or poor
- those who change in some way/don't change .

4 Consider if there is a connection between these judgements you have just made, the themes, and how the writer is influencing the audience to respond to these issues.

## Activity 3.7.1

Working in groups, discuss how the following paragraph:

- links theme to character
- summarises the writer's main message about this issue.

*Social class is one of the themes of Willy Russell's play* Blood Brothers. *Through her actions and speech it is clear that the character, Mrs Lyons, is being presented as a snob who uses her money to exploit her socially deprived cleaner, Mrs Johnstone. Mrs Lyons also takes advantage of the fact that the poorly educated Mrs Johnstone is superstitious to frighten her when she changes her mind about giving her one of the twins. She uses a feeble excuse to get rid of her, saying her work has 'deteriorated' and there is nothing Mrs Johnstone can do about it. She is powerless in the face of the superiority of Mrs Lyons' money and social standing. The fact that the policeman treats the two families so differently when the boys get into trouble further highlights what the playwright clearly considers to be the underlying unfairness and prejudice of the class system.*

## Activity 3.7.2

Choose a theme from the play you are studying and assess how a character or characters contribute to its development in the play. Use the paragraph in Activity 3.7.1 as a model. Your task is to work together to write a similar piece which outlines the relationship between your selected theme and characters, and which sums up the writer's main message.

A spokesperson from each group could read the completed piece to the rest of the class and other members of the group will respond to any questions that arise.

*Note*: If you are studying *Blood Brothers,* choose a different theme and characters from those used in the above example.

## The Assessment Objectives for drama texts

The first chapter has outlined the significance of Assessment Objectives and explained their centrality to the examining process: their function need not be discussed again. The relevant objectives are a summary of the skills and abilities that you are expected to show in the examination. Take comfort from the knowledge that if your response is relevant, then you will demonstrate these skills and abilities.

Here is a brief summary of what is expected to be found in an answer:

- **AO 1** requires that candidates present a **personal response** and **informed argument**
- **AO 2** obliges the student to demonstrate **an understanding of the dramatist's methods and intentions**.

## How to unpack the question

In common with the other two sections of this examination, you will have a choice of two possible questions:

- Question (a) will focus on **character**.
- Question (b) will focus on a **theme** or **issue**.

Foundation and Higher Tier papers use the same structure to present both these questions. There will, however, be subtle differences in the wording used. Foundation Tier papers offer further clarification and more straightforward language/terminology, as highlighted below:

Question 2(a) *Higher Tier*

**This question is about Mrs Birling.**

Look again at the extract beginning at the top of page 46 with Mrs Birling's words, 'Oh, stop it, both of you' and ending at the end of Act 2.

From the way Priestley **presents** Mrs Birling in the extract and elsewhere in the play, show how far you would agree that she is an **unfeeling** character.

*(From 2006)*

Question 2(a) *Foundation Tier*

**This question is about Mrs Birling.**

Look again at the extract beginning at the top of page 46 with Mrs Birling's words, 'Oh, stop it, both of you' and ending at the top of page 49, with the Inspector's words, 'To do my duty.'

From the way Priestley **presents** Mrs Birling in the extract and elsewhere in the play, show that she is an **unfeeling woman** who does not care for other people.

*(From 2006)*

Both tiers of entry employ the same basic format to structure the questions in this section. It is important, therefore, that you familiarise yourself with this layout at an early stage in your course, as this will be invaluable in helping you to navigate your way around the questions under examination conditions.

A typical question is 'unpacked' for you below:

This instruction is to help you locate the extract which you have to consider initially and analyse in light of the question.

Key words will be highlighted in bold print.

Note how the final bullet point directs you to consider the issue beyond the extract.

Friel: *Dancing at Lughnasa*

5(b) **This question is about a sense of unease.**

Look again at the extract beginning at the top of page 56 with Kate's words, 'What do you know about this Bradley business?' and ending with in the middle of page 59 when Rose exits.

From the way Friel **presents** the Mundy sisters in the extract and from what the older Michael says elsewhere in the play, show that there is a **sense of unease** among them.

In your answer, you should consider:

- the sisters' words and behaviour in the extract
- Friel's use of stage directions in the extract
- what the older Michael says about the atmosphere in the Mundy sisters' household elsewhere in the play.

(You should spend no longer than 50 minutes on this question.)

The focus of the task will always be in bold print on the first line. It is highlighted in this way because this is what should be at the heart of your answer.

This is the task you are to complete in the time specified. The core of the question is revealed – in this case, pinpointing how the presentation of the Mundy sisters reveals the unease among them.

This is advice you should not ignore. Timing is vital to maximise success in any examination.

By addressing these bullet points, you will build a relevant answer.

As you go on to look at the **sample answers** that follow, it is worth checking out how far the various bits of advice about intelligent unpacking of questions were actually taken on board by these candidates.

## Sample answers

This was a response to a question from the 2005 Higher Tier paper:

1(a) Wilder: *Our Town* – the question is about **valuing life**

*Wilder portrays the idea that life is not valued while it is lived the whole way through the play, as it is the main, most important theme throughout. He wants us to feel that we often take life for granted and it is too late when we are dead to do anything about it but to feel regret. This is conveyed when Emily says 'I can't. I can't go on. It goes too fast. We don't have time to look at one another.' This shows that Emily did not realise how special life really was until she had lost it.*

The candidate starts by focusing on the question and then begins to address the first bullet point at the end of the paragraph.

*Simon Stimson, another character, feels the same way as he claims 'Now you know! That's what it was to be alive. To move about in a cloud of ignorance.' This shows that he is also regretful of his actions when he had once lived. Before he had died Simon Stimson was a man who is seen to waste his life and is talked about by the people living close to him. We learn this from earlier on in the play when Mrs Soames says, 'But, Julia! To have the organist of a church drink and drunk year after year.' This proves that there must be a great truth behind what Simon Stimson claims when he is dead as he knows what it is like to regret having spent nearly his whole life drinking alcohol.*

Some apt textual details regarding what is learnt about Simon Stimson elsewhere in the play.

A valid interpretation but could be further developed.

*Emily puts across the point of us not valuing life enough when she sobs, 'Oh, Earth, you're too wonderful for anybody to realise you.' This makes the audience realise too just how much ignorance there is in today's society. Not only do the characters believe it but it makes the people watching the play see the importance of how we act towards our everyday lives. So the point is put across very strongly.*

Another appropriate observation which keeps the question in focus.

*When Emily revisits her twelfth birthday, her reactions show just how much she loved being alive and how much she had forgotten about. 'And, look, there's the old whole fence that used to be around our house. Oh, I'd forgotten that! Oh, I love it so!' In doing this the message is conveyed in an even stronger light, as the smallest things such as a fence can make us happy without us realising it. If subjects like this are taken for granted, so must a lot of other things. She also says, 'I can't bear it. I love you all, everything – I can't look at everything hard enough.' This point confirms it for her that we abuse everything about life by acting as if we don't have it and that it means nothing when, in reality, it does.*

In this paragraph the candidate deals with the second bullet point and offers a reasonably detailed interpretation of the incident.

*The stage manager is a multi-dimensional character. He plays different roles and talks to the audience as if they are his friends. He is able to tell us when times have changed,*

The candidate now turns his/her attention to the fourth bullet point, demonstrating an understanding of the stage manager's role in conveying the message that life is not valued while it is lived.

*when people have given birth or died. He tells us the name of the town is Grover's Corners, New Hampshire – just across the Massachusetts line. This fact of where they live shows that Grover's Corners is just a small town, like many others in the world. This therefore helps us to see that when he talks about the events that happen, they are not just things happening in that town but all around the world. In Grover's Corners as we have seen, life is not valued while it is lived. So if it is happening in this town then that leads us to think more about how it affects the rest of the world. The truth is that in the rest of the world other people are exactly the same. The stage manager's role is one of the most important in the play as he makes living people realise just how precious life and living really is. He puts across the message to the audience in order to make them see, before it is too late.*

The conclusion offers a relevant summation of the play's main message. →

*Overall, this play has a lot of truth in it, even though nothing spectacular happens. Its message is put across very strongly, and this Simon Stimson describes as 'ignorance and blindness'. We are too concerned about other things to appreciate what we have. We do not enjoy life due to our blindness of it while we are living.*

## Activity 3.9.1

The answer you've just read was awarded a mark towards the top of Band 3. Its strengths were that focus on the question was sustained and that all bullet points were referred to. There were, however, missed opportunities to offer a much more detailed analysis of each of the bullet points.

Your challenge is to revamp the piece. First of all, decide what further arguments, interpretations and textual references could be added to achieve this. Next, write a new improved version of the original answer.

## Activity 3.9.2

Re-read the section on pages 2 and 3 to remind you how Mark Bands are used, and then use the complete Assessment Matrix on page 74 to mark a revised essay written by one of your classmates in response to Activity 3.9.1.

Your comments must justify the mark you award - hopefully from Mark Bands 4 or 5.

The following is a response to a question from the 2005 Foundation paper:

3(a) Friel: *Dancing at Lughnasa* – the question is about **dancing**

*Gerry's and Chris's dance in the play is a slow dance. 'He suddenly swings her round and round and dances her lightly, elegantly across the garden.' There dance is very slow and it is the kind of dance were you let the person who you are dancing with know how much you love them 'Marry me, Chrissie.' Then Gerry and Chris dance off somewhere else.*

*Maggie starts to dance in the kitchen to the radio first. 'At the same time she opens her mouth and emits an instant raucous Yaaah! And immediately begins to dance.' She dances with her arms, legs, hair and long boot laces flying and then Rosie starts to dance with her.' Then Rose starts to dance with her and they sing and shout together. Rose's Wellingtons were pounding out their own erratic rhythm. Then Agnes leaps up and joins them. Agnes moves most gracefully and sensuously out of all the sisters. After the interval Chris joins in they are all dancing now. Then Kate gets up and starts dancing alone, totally concentrated and totally private. Kate starts dancing around the house very excited making no sound while the rest of the sisters are singing and shouting together.*

*Gerry starts to dance with Agnes when they got the radio working again. 'With style and with easy elegance they dance one another around the kitchen and then out to the garden.' This dance is another slow dance it is very relaxing. Gerry starts to dance Agnes back into the kitchen then they stop.*

The candidate offers some basic comment about how Gerry and Chris are feeling.

The candidate attempts to deal with the second bullet point but the approach is narrative. There is no awareness of dramatic techniques and only some awareness of the significance of this event.

There is a brief effort to offer a simple comment in the midst of the reporting of the dancing.

### Activity 3.9.3

The above answer does attempt to focus on the question, but with limited success. This is because the candidate has, for the most part, simply described a couple of occasions when different characters danced in the play.

Using the Assessment Matrix on page 74, decide which Mark Band and what score this response should be awarded. You must be able to justify your decisions.

On the next page is another essay in response to the same question. This candidate has been much more successful in addressing the question. Read the essay and then try the activity that follows:

3(a) Friel: *Dancing at Lughnasa* – the question is about **dancing**

*'Dancing at Lughnasa' is a play where the sisters do not verbally communicate with each other well. This makes the subtext almost as important as what is actually said. Throughout the play, the medium of dance is used at several significant moments to say more than speech ever could.*

*In this extract Gerry and Chris are blissfully enjoying a dance together. Gerry is a character who tries to charm women and, at this point, that is what he is doing. He is asking Chris to leave with him and he knows the only thing he 'could ever do well – was dance'. Chris is besotted with him and his dance is used to 'woo' her and make her more relaxed with him.*

*Kate sees them dancing and is appalled. The play is set in 1936 when religion was taken very seriously. Kate, being a very religious woman, sees them dancing as a pagan tradition that 'mature women' like themselves should not do. She is also afraid that Gerry is leading Chris on and that she will fall more deeply in love with him. She is the protector in the house and although she is highly critical of Gerry's motives, she grants her sister a few minutes happiness out of love for her.*

*When the sisters dance to the radio together Friel shows us a wide range of attitudes. Maggie, who has always been the more outgoing sister, starts dancing before anyone else. She is not as strictly confined to convention as the rest of the sisters. She does not care if dancing is seen as a pagan tradition. Maggie practically induces a pagan element to the dance by putting white flour on her face like a 'mask'. Next, it is Rose who joins her. Rose has learning disabilities and is seen as a threat because of her lack of control. She has no boundaries in her actions and therefore dances to suit her attitude towards it. She has her 'own erratic rhythm'.*

*The actions of Chris are very significant in this dance. As she had a child out of wedlock, she has been held down by religious hypocrisy. By flinging Jack's surplice over her head during the dance, she is making a stand of showing her unleashed frustration of the hypocrisy, despite Kate's protests.*

*In this dance Kate is the last to get up and, when she does, she dances alone. Even throughout her contradiction of what she believes in, she excludes herself. Her dance is strict and 'controlled' like her. It symbolises her objective not to break boundaries and to remain repressed by Irish society.*

*The order in which the sisters stop dancing represents the extent of their repression and how they feel about dancing. Kate prefers to express herself verbally and stops first whereas Rose does not have the intellect to do so and is last to finish. Through this dance Friel shows us the different thoughts and feelings of the sisters towards dancing. The sisters who are less repressed by convention are the ones more accepting of dance.*

*Another important dance is the one between Agnes and Gerry. There has always been an implication in the play that Agnes harbours a secret infatuation for Gerry. When he is dancing with Chris she does not watch but shouts, 'For God's sake can't you see I'm busy!' Gerry is aware of this because he asks Chris to send his love to Agnes earlier in the play. Gerry enjoys charming women and shows this when he asks Agnes to dance. Maggie, unaware of Agnes' feelings convinces her to dance, whereas Chris is not happy about it. She knows Gerry for what he is and is jealous when he and Agnes dance.*

*Friel is showing us the power of dance and how it affects the characters who dance in different ways. At this point to Maggie it is just a bit of fun but to Agnes it will be a chance to feel more heartache. Gerry sees it as a chance to charm Agnes and Chris is jealous because she knows Gerry will never just be hers.*

*In this play Friel shows the devastating effects of lack of communication but he also highlights the importance of dance and the differing thoughts and feelings of the characters towards dancing.*

### Activity 3.9.4

In groups, discuss and decide on the following:

- What has this candidate done that makes it a better answer than the previous response (on page 24)?
- Can you identify any weaknesses in this essay?
- What other points/examples could be added in answer to the question?
- Using the Assessment Matrix on page 74, agree a mark. Remember that you must be able to justify this mark.
- Finally, write down the comment you feel this candidate deserves, praising the essay's strengths and highlighting any areas for improvement.

## Some practice questions

Here are some practice questions on the most popular drama texts. There is a Foundation Tier and a Higher Tier question in each case. Remember that the bullet points are prompts that are there to help you to produce a relevant answer. As these practice questions are assessing drama, frequently one of the bullet points will focus on stage directions and dramatic techniques. It is easy to overlook these in this, the open book section, of the exam.

In Chapter 6 you will find a checklist of possible points for each of these questions.

### Wilder: *Our Town*

### Activity 3.10.1

*Higher Tier*

**This question is about the Stage Manager.**

Look again at the extract that begins on page 66 with the Stage Manager's words: 'This time nine years have gone by …' and ends on page 69 with the words '… that left town to go west.'

From what you read in the extract and elsewhere in the play, show your understanding of the **contribution the Stage Manager makes** to what happens.

In your answer you should consider:

- how he controls time
- how he interacts with the audience
- how he interacts with the other characters.

### Activity 3.10.2

*Foundation Tier*

**This question is about love.**

Look again at the extract that begins on page 55 with George's words 'Emily, I'm glad you spoke to me …' and ends on page 58 with the Stage Manager's words ''Twan't very long anyway.'

From what you read in the extract and elsewhere in the play, show how the writer **presents** different **kinds of love**.

In your answer, you should consider what is revealed:

- about the feelings George and Emily have for each other in the extract
- through Wilder's use of stage directions and dramatic techniques in the extract
- about the importance of family life in Act 1
- about how important it is to love life in Act 3.

## Russell: *Blood Brothers*

### Activity 3.11.1

*Higher Tier*

**This question is about parenthood.**

Look again at the extract beginning on page 7 with Mrs Johnstone's words 'With one more baby we could have managed' and ending at the bottom of page 10 when Mrs Lyons says 'I want it to look right before I go shopping.'

From the way Russell **presents** the two women in the extract and elsewhere in the play, who do you think makes **the better parent**?

In your answer, you should consider:

- what the two women say and how they behave in the extract
- what you learn elsewhere in Act 1 about how Mrs Johnstone brings up her family
- what you learn elsewhere in the play about the relationship between Mrs Lyons and Edward
- who is to blame for the twins' death and anything else you think is relevant.

### Activity 3.11.2

*Foundation Tier*

**This question is about Mickey and Edward's friendship.**

Look again at the extract beginning on page 23 with the stage direction 'Edward also aged seven appears. He is bright and forthcoming' and ending on page 26 with the stage direction 'Sammy leaps in front of them, gun in hand, pointed at them.'

From the way Russell **presents** Mickey and Edward in the extract and elsewhere in the play, what do you learn about their **friendship** and how **it changes**?

In your answer, you should consider the following:

- what they say and do when they first meet in the extract
- how their friendship builds up in Act 1
- why the brothers grow apart and eventually die together in Act 2
- anything else you think is relevant.

## Friel: *Dancing at Lughnasa*

### Activity 3.12.1

*Higher Tier*

**This question is about the family relationships.**

Look again at the extract beginning on page 42 with Kate's words 'I haven't seen her' and ending on page 46 with 'Mother of God, will we ever be able to lift our heads ever again ... ?'

From the way Friel **presents** the sisters in the extract and elsewhere in the play, show your understanding about how the sisters **relate to one another**.

In your answer, you should consider:

- what they say and do in the extract
- Friel's use of stage directions and dramatic techniques in the extract
- what the older Michael says about the sisters elsewhere in the play
- anything else you think is relevant.

### Activity 3.12.2

*Foundation Tier*

**This question is about Gerry.**

Look again at the extract that begins on page 26 with the stage direction 'Gerry Evans enters L …' and ends on page 31 with Gerry's words 'With your eyes lucky boy.'

From the way Friel **presents** Gerry Evans in the extract and elsewhere in the play, what do you learn about **the kind of person he is**?

In your answer, you should consider:

- what he says to Chris in the extract
- the reactions of the sisters to Gerry in the extract and elsewhere in the play
- Gerry's behaviour elsewhere in the play
- anything else you think is relevant.

# Priestley: *An Inspector Calls*

## Activity 3.13.1

*Higher Tier*

**This question is about Mr Birling.**

Look again at the extract beginning on page 8 with the stage direction 'Edna takes the Inspector's hat and coat and goes out' and ends on page 11 with Birling's words 'I didn't suppose you did.'

From the way Priestley **presents** Mr Birling here and elsewhere in the play, how far would you agree that he is a man who **cares only for himself and his reputation?**

In your answer, you should consider:

- Mr Birling's speech and behaviour in the extract
- how the Inspector reacts towards Mr Birling in the extract
- Priestley's use of stage directions in the extract
- any other relevant examples elsewhere in the play.

## Activity 3.13.2

*Foundation Tier*

**This question is about Birling family life.**

Look again at the extract that begins on page 42 with the stage direction 'He walks straight out, leaving them staring, subdued and wondering' and ends on page 44 with Birling's words '… and get to work quickly too.'

From what you read in the extract and elsewhere in the play, would you agree that the writer **presents** the Birling family as **bitter and hard towards others**?

In your answer you should consider:

- what the family say and how they behave in the extract
- their attitude to the Inspector in the extract and elsewhere in the play
- how Eva Smith is treated elsewhere in the play.

# Chapter 4: The prose section

## Studying prose texts

It is hoped that most of you who are studying this GCSE English Literature course are doing so mainly because you like reading. Most of us buy or borrow a novel, a work of fiction, for pleasure, to enjoy a 'good read'. We usually know the sort of novel we want to read: it may have been recommended by friends, it may tie in with a film we have seen, or it may have been written by an author whose work we enjoy. In the end, when we look back on a novel we have read it is the story itself that we probably remember best.

### Activity 4.1

Working in pairs, think of a novel you really enjoyed reading. Then outline for your partner:

- the **main stages** in the storyline
- the **best moment** in the story.

While the study of a GCSE English Literature prose text should ideally begin with that natural enjoyment of the storyline, of course there is much more to the study of a prose text for examination. Success in this exam does not solely depend on how well you 'know the story', although that is important and does form the necessary foundation on which you have to build all the other skills involved in analysing and evaluating a prose text.

For example, you will have to consider these two important questions:

- **Why** did the author write this text?

  You need to be aware of the **themes or issues** that he/she wanted to explore.

- **How** did the author write it?

  You have to be able to identify and comment on the various **skills and techniques** used by the writer to make the story really interesting, such as character development or use of language.

In other words, when studying a text for examination you are expected to show close engagement with all aspects of that text and show an awareness and understanding of the writer's purpose and skills.

## Key features of prose texts

Before arriving in the examination hall, you need to have a thorough, detailed knowledge and understanding of the text. This will arise from classroom experiences, personal study, essay practice and revision, and perhaps also internet research. If you are going to discuss and evaluate a novel thoroughly, the most important aspects of a text are:

- **setting** – the situation in which the story takes place
- **plot** – the sequence of events that forms the storyline

- **themes** – the important issues that the author wants to explore
- **characters** – and the relationships between them
- **language and style** – use of dialogue, similes/metaphors, colloquial language, etc.

## Setting

A writer always sets his/her story in a specific place or against a certain background for particular reasons. For example, in *Of Mice and Men* John Steinbeck sets his story against the background of the tough life on a ranch at the time of the Great Depression in America in the 1930s. This enables him to show vividly the grim conditions that travelling labourers had to endure at that time.

Remember that in some cases authors will include more than one distinct setting in their stories, for purposes of contrast.

### Activity 4.2

In pairs or groups, consider your prose text in order to:

- identify in a series of bullet points, the **main locations** used throughout your novel
- outline the main **reasons why** you think the writer has chosen these settings.

## Plot

As we've already established, the plot in a prose text is the linked sequence of events that provides the basic foundation of the story. The plot is, in a way, the 'skeleton' of the prose text, the bones onto which writers build the complex 'flesh' of their creations.

In some cases, the plot of a prose text is fairly straightforward and based on a time sequence. For example, the plot of George Orwell's *Animal Farm* is a chronological, step-by-step account of how life changes for the animals over a number of years. In other cases, the plot may not be so straightforward and may involve the use of flashbacks for example.

Writers often like to increase the suspense or add to the mystery of a story by developing unusual twists and turns in the plot, in order to sustain the reader's interest. You need to be aware of the purpose and effect of such plot devices.

The most important stage of the plot is usually the final part, the **climax** of the story, the moment when the writer wants to make his/her point, or reveal the most important development, most dramatically and effectively. For example, in *Animal Farm*, the climax is where we read how Benjamin and Clover – looking in the window at the celebratory banquet in the farmhouse – glance from pig to man, and from man to pig, and realise that they cannot tell the difference? This is the final dramatic revelation for the suffering 'lower' animals: pigs and men are indistinguishable, and equally corrupt.

### Activity 4.3

In groups, in the case of your text, discuss and agree on:

- the most interesting, exciting or unusual parts of the plot
- exactly where the **climax** of the story comes.

Report back and discuss the different findings.

## Themes

Writers have very clear purposes in creating a best-selling novel – purposes other than simply giving the public 'a good read' or, more honestly, making some money for themselves!

We would certainly like to think that there is a 'serious purpose' behind the story, that the writer wants to illustrate his/her views on a particular issue or, more cleverly, manipulate readers' attitudes towards that issue. For example, in *To Kill a Mockingbird*, Harper Lee wants to expose the problems arising from racial prejudice in the American 'Deep South' and to make her readers feel sympathy for victims of such prejudice.

Writers, however, frequently explore more than one theme in their story and often present a range of ideas and attitudes about the way people live.

### Activity 4.4

Whole-class 'brainstorming' exercise/group presentation:

- Through the use of a flipchart/whiteboard, identify the **main themes** touched on by the writer of your text.
- Having identified these themes, in groups, consider what messages the writer wishes to convey about his/her themes.

## Characters

Characters in a prose text do not invent themselves, nor are they people whom the writer accidentally stumbled upon! They are deliberately created, shaped and perfected in the writer's imagination, and the writer only allows us to see them as he/she intends us to see them.

We therefore need to be aware of the ways writers create and develop characters for us and how they manipulate our feelings about those characters.

We can develop an insight into characters in a prose text by assessing:

- what they look like
- what they do
- what they say (and how they say it!)
- what they think and feel
- what other people say about them
- how other people treat them or react to them

but also through:

- **how the writer influences our attitudes** towards them – for example, through the language or the images used to present them. Note, for instance, how in *Of Mice and Men* Steinbeck helps us to understand Lennie through linking him with animals.

### Activity 4.5

Pair/group work. Focusing on one major character in your text and using the bullet points on page 32:

- discuss how the writer tries to **manipulate** your thoughts about him or her
- identify in simple bullet points the **ways** in which the writer does this.

## Language and style

Every writer chooses a distinctive **style** of writing to suit:

- his/her chosen setting
- the characters he/she presents
- the sort of story he/she is telling
- what is happening in the story at a particular stage.

The language and style of a prose text can include a wide range of features. For example:

- **narrative stance** – the point of view from which the story is told. For example, *To Kill a Mockingbird* and *How Many Miles to Babylon?* are presented in the **first person**, through the eyes of one of the characters in the novel. The writer has **adopted the persona** of a character, and the effect of this is to draw the reader more intimately into the events of the story, which makes it somehow more personal and immediate. On the other hand, *Lord of the Flies* and *I'm the King of the Castle* are presented in the **third person**, through the eyes of an outside observer. The writer in such cases therefore seems more detached and objective in his/her presentation of the story.
- vivid **adjectives** or **descriptive phrases** – the description of the tropical island in *Lord of the Flies*: 'Here and there, *little breezes* crept over *the polished waters* beneath the *haze of heat*. When these breezes reached the platform the *palm-fronds would whisper*, so that *spots of blurred sunlight* slid over their bodies *or moved like bright, winged things* in the shade.'
- **similes and metaphors** – in *Of Mice and Men*, Slim's '*hatchet face* was ageless' or in *How Many Miles to Babylon?*, 'the Major's voice *like a sharp metal probe* touched a nerve in my brain.'
- use of **dialogue** – for example, the tense dialogue between Kingshaw and Hooper in Chapter 12 of *I'm the King of the Castle*.
- use of **symbols** – the *conch* or the *pig's head* in *Lord of the Flies*.

- **verbs of action/violence** – in *To Kill a Mockingbird*, consider the description of the shooting of the mad dog: 'Atticus's hand *yanked* a ball-tipped lever as he brought the gun to his shoulder. The rifle *cracked*. Tim Johnson *leaped, flopped over* and *crumpled* on the sidewalk in a brown and white heap.'
- use of **dialect/colloquial expressions** – in *Of Mice and Men*, Candy 'said excitedly, "We *oughtta let 'im* get away. Curly *go'n'ta wanta* get 'im lynched."'
- the **building of tension** – especially towards the end of a chapter or an important event. In *Lord of the Flies*, at the end of Chapter 11, the writer hints at the violence that Sam and Eric are about to endure: 'Roger edged past the Chief, only just avoiding pushing him with his shoulder. The *yelling ceased*, and Samneric lay looking up in *quiet terror*. Roger *advanced upon them* as one wielding a *nameless authority*.'

## Activity 4.6

In pairs or groups, consider the range of writers' techniques Jennifer Johnson has used below in the opening two paragraphs of her novel *How Many Miles to Babylon?*

Use the following questions to guide you:

- At what point in the sequence of events do you suspect she has chosen to begin the story?
- What narrative stance has she employed?
- How has the writer drawn the reader into her story in these two opening paragraphs?

Because I am an officer and a gentleman they have given me my notebooks, pen, ink and paper. So I write and wait. I am committed to no cause, I love no living person. The fact that I have no future except what you can count in hours doesn't disturb me unduly. After all, the future whether here or there is equally unknown. So for the waiting days I have only the past to play about with. I can juggle with a series of possibly inaccurate memories, my own interpretation, for what it is worth, of events. Strangely enough I think I like that.

I have not communicated with either my father or mother. Time enough for others to do that when it is over. The fait accompli. On His Majesty's Service. Why prolong the pain they will inevitably feel? It may kill him, but then, like me, he may be better off dead. My heart doesn't bleed for her.

*How Many Miles to Babylon?*

# The Assessment Objectives for prose texts

The Assessment Objectives provide an indication of the skills and abilities that you are expected to demonstrate in the examination.

## AO 1

Candidates are required to respond to texts **critically**, **sensitively and in detail**, selecting **appropriate ways to convey their response**, using **textual evidence** as appropriate.

In order to meet this assessment objective, you must be able to:

- offer a **personal response** to the text rather than merely retell the story!
- present **informed argument** based on the question set – develop relevant ideas
- use appropriate **literary terms/language** when discussing the text and be able to *recognise the effect* of literary devices such as similes, metaphors, etc.
- refer to **relevant parts of the text** and sometimes **use quotations** to illustrate the points you are making – back up your argument with evidence.

These requirements may sound difficult and demanding, but if you have a **thorough knowledge** of the text and an **interest in the characters and themes** it presents, you should have no problem presenting an appropriate response.

Look at how the following example covers all the requirements of AO 1 in one paragraph. The question is about how characters (George and Lennie) in *Of Mice and Men* show different types of power.

Clear personal response to the character.

References to examples in the text.

Further textual reference to back up point about his strength.

*Lennie is a powerful and destructive figure in the novel; he is unaware of his great strength and cannot control it. We see this in the way he often kills mice by stroking them and in the way he accidentally kills the puppy that was given to him. His terrible strength is also seen when he accidentally kills Curley's wife at the end of the story. The horror of this incident and the extent of his physical power is reflected in the simile describing how her body 'flopped like a fish' when he shook her. However, most of the time Lennie is a gentle giant. He allows himself to be led and guided by his workmate George who is a much smaller man, but who has 'dark eyes and strong, sharp features.' He exerts a powerful influence over Lennie for much of the time and Lennie sees him as a father figure.*

Recognises the purpose of the simile – using quotation effectively.

Informed argument – developing ideas about the character.

## AO 2

Candidates are required to explore how **language, structure and forms contribute to the meanings** of texts, considering **different approaches** to texts and **alternative interpretations**.

To meet this assessment objective, you must demonstrate to the examiner that you have a clear understanding of:

- the **writer's methods** and the effects used – the various features of his/her 'style'
- the **writer's intentions** – the 'meanings' he/she wants us to see in the text, the way in he/she **wants us to react** to characters or situations
- the range of **differing opinions** readers can have about characters or situations – there is not one correct view to have about an aspect of a text. Each reader will have his/her individual reaction to a character or an event.

Again look at how these requirements can be demonstrated to some extent in one paragraph. The focus of the paragraph is Piggy in *Lord of the Flies*.

*From the start of the novel, Golding wants us to see that Piggy is different from the other boys, an outsider who is never fully accepted into the group. He makes him different by emphasising his physical weakness and his disabilities – he has very poor eyesight and suffers from asthma. Few of the others have any sympathy for Piggy and even Ralph, who is naturally kind and tolerates him most of the time, says to him, 'Sucks to your ass-mar!', mocking both his ailment and his accent. Jack, the villain of the story, has no time for the whingeing Piggy and on more than one occasion 'mimicked his whine'. The writer seems to deliberately make him look like a pig and sound like a pig, with his constant whining, squealing and protesting. He becomes a figure that others treat with contempt and scorn. However, although most readers at times find Piggy a weak, ineffective and frustrating character, it is clear that he is intelligent and far-seeing, and understands the horrors that lie ahead, if the boys do not establish a disciplined society on the island. When he is so brutally removed from the scene near the end of the novel, the endangered and isolated Ralph deeply regrets that there is now 'no Piggy to talk sense.'*

Recognises the writer's intention – to make us see Piggy as different.

Awareness of a method the writer uses to emphasise a feature of his character.

Aware of how the writer makes the others treat Piggy with contempt.

Demonstrates a clear awareness of the differing opinions of the character.

Appropriate use of neatly embedded quotation.

# What the examiner is looking for – key indicators in the Mark Scheme

It is important to realise that the examiners are not concerned with finding out what students do not know – they are not trying to 'catch you out'! Examiners aim to reward students for presenting what they **do know**. Obviously, the more you know and understand a prose text, and the more convincingly and fluently you can present an organised response to a question on it, the higher the mark you will be awarded. The precise mark you achieve for your essay will depend on how fully you have met the two Assessment Objectives outlined in the previous section.

As you have already seen in Chapter 1, the Assessment Objectives are measured using an **Assessment Matrix**. This enables the examiner to judge the quality of your essay, measured against descriptions outlined for 'bands' or levels of response in each Assessment Objective.

Below is the Assessment Matrix used for the Higher Tier Prose question. The Foundation Tier matrix is similar, the only difference being that there is no Band 5 at this tier.

| **Assessment Objective** | **Band 1 Marks 0–5** | **Band 2 Marks 6–15** | **Band 3 Marks 16–25** | **Band 4 Marks 26–30** | **Band 5 Marks 31–35** |
|---|---|---|---|---|---|
| **AO 1 Argument** | Some writing about text or task. | Simple, straight forward or limited response.<br>Attempt to focus on question.<br>Assertion, basic conclusion, narrative or description. | Begins to develop a response. / Fairly developed response.<br>Begins to focus on question. / Some focus on question.<br>Some argument. | Reasoned response.<br>Sustained focus on question.<br>Developed argument. | Evaluative response.<br>Persuasive, coherent answer to the question.<br>Sustained argument. |
| **AO 2 Form and Language** | Simplistic comments about characters, setting and events.<br>Little or no awareness of structure, form or prose techniques. | Some awareness of significance of characters, setting and events.<br>Some awareness of structure, form or prose techniques.<br>Occasional reference to the writer's words. | Comments on characters, setting and events.<br>Comments on structure, form or prose techniques.<br>Some understanding of the writer's use of language. | Interpretation of characters, setting and events.<br>Some discussion on the effects of structure, form or prose techniques.<br>Meaningful comment on some stylistic devices, with the emergence of a critical vocabulary. | Assured interpretation of characters, setting and events.<br>Developed discussion on the effects of structure, form or prose techniques.<br>Analysis of the writer's language and style, using appropriate critical terminology. |

If you want to be successful in the examination, this Matrix shows you that you have to:

- give a **personal response** to the text
- be **relevant**, focusing precisely on the **question set**
- develop a **consistent argument** in response to the question set
- comment on **characters, setting and events**
- show awareness of the **literary devices** the writer is using
- comment on how the writer **uses language**.

Of course, each of these requirements does not have to be demonstrated to an equal extent during the course of your essay. Depending on the question set, there may be a particular focus on one or two of them.

Again, these requirements sound demanding, but they can be demonstrated to the examiner fairly easily in the course of a thoughtful and engaged response.

Look at the following extract from a sample essay. Here, the question ('To what extent do you think that Major Glendinning is the villain of the novel?') is based on *How Many Miles to Babylon?*

*... If not the villain of the story, Major Glendinning is certainly a cold, cruel and ruthless character, and as a commanding officer he rules his men with an iron fist and harsh discipline. He does not make 'idle threats' and on one occasion struck Lieutenant Moore viciously across the face with his cane when he said something insolent. He drives his men into action through fear, telling them he will have 'no scruples about handing out the ultimate' punishment. He proves this towards the end of the story when he has Private Crowe sentenced to death for supposedly deserting his post. He has little sympathy for the sufferings his soldiers have to endure in the mud and horror of the trenches and looks on them with contempt, openly telling them that they are a 'sorry lot'. His cruel nature is symbolised by the way he is often associated with the pocket knife which he always carries, using it to peel an apple carefully and precisely, or to end the sufferings of a mortally wounded soldier, abandoned in a shell hole.*

*However, it is difficult to interpret him as entirely a villain. He displays personal bravery and does in fact lead from the front; it is he who leads the dangerous mission to 'see to' the wounded soldier. He is the one who has to undertake the really difficult tasks and in the darkness and confusion of the shell hole in no-man's land, while the sensitive, horror-struck Lieutenant Moore is incapable of firm action, it is the Major who has to do the grim but necessary deed. Also, behind the man of steel there is on occasions a glimpse of a softer side. For example ...*

In this sample response, the candidate has covered most of the requirements in the Assessment Objectives, to some extent:

✓ There is a **clear, personal response** to the text, where the candidate asserts that Major Glendinning can not be interpreted as 'entirely a villain'.

✓ The commentary is wholly **relevant**, focusing on whether or not Major Glendinning is a villain.

✓ The argument is **consistent** and quite **confident**. The candidate is **developing and sustaining an argument** that there are two different sides to the Major.

✓ There is clear comment on **characters** (Lieutenant is 'sensitive' and 'horror-struck'), a reference to the **setting** (mud and horror of the trenches) and **events** (a reference to the sentencing of Private Crowe).

✓ There is some awareness of **literary devices** used by the writer (the understanding that the knife is used as a **symbol** of the Major's cruelty).

✓ There is an understanding of **how language can be used** (noting that the writer shows Major Glendinning's contempt for his men by using the term a 'sorry lot').

As illustrated here, you need not be afraid of the Assessment Matrix! If you have a thorough understanding of the text and engage with the set question in a sustained and relevant manner, you will cover the main requirements.

## Activity 4.7

Group work. This candidate has performed well. Use the Matrix on page 37 to agree:

- the **band** into which you think this segment falls
- the actual **mark** you would give it within that band.

Groups should then report back to see if there is general agreement!

As well as the Assessment Matrix, examiners are also given some indication of the sort of ideas/arguments/references that might occur in a response to the given question. As well as these possible responses, they will also credit other relevant and appropriately argued ideas offered by individual candidates.

For example, look at the beginning of a typical question on *Of Mice and Men*.

To what extent do you think that Steinbeck presents **Crooks** as a character **to be pitied**?

In the Mark Scheme, examiners might be told that some of the following points could be raised in students' answers:

- He is segregated from the other ranch-hands, **living on his own**.
- He suffers **racial prejudice**, as he tells Lennie he's not allowed to play cards in the bunkhouse because he's black.
- He is **disabled**, he's described as a 'cripple' – he has a problem with his spine.
- On the ranch, he is given the **most menial tasks** to do.
- He **works most of the time with the animals** on the farm and has little contact with humans.
- He is **denied access to George and Lennie's dream** of a farm of their own.
- He is **at the mercy of Curley's wife** – 'I could get you strung up on a tree so easy it ain't even funny.'
- He **endures aggression** from others – we are told of a fight he has with Smitty at Christmas. Candy describes it as 'fun'.

This list is not intended to be comprehensive. These are only suggestions and it is possible to refer to other equally valid aspects of Crooks' life.

**Activity 4.8**

Group work. Your teacher will select **one character** from your prose text for each group.

Your task is to:

- Decide how you think your character has been portrayed by the writer. (Someone to be admired, pitied or hated perhaps?)
- Using the 'Crooks' list' as a model, make a **bullet point list of your conclusions and the evidence** upon which they are based.
- Share these ideas with the other groups.

# How to unpack essay questions

## Choosing the question

In the case of all the prescribed prose texts in this examination, there is a choice between either Question (a) or (b).

In most instances, the choice is generally between:

- a **character-focused** essay – you have to present your ideas about that character, in response to the specific question set.

  or

- a **theme-focused** essay – you have to write about how the writer explores a particular theme or issue that is a strong feature of the text. You will already know from a detailed study of your text what major themes are raised in it.

Look at these two questions on *How Many Miles to Babylon?*

> (a) **This question is about Alexander.**
>
> Show how far you would agree that Alexander is an **isolated** character.
>
> In your answer, you should consider:
> - his life in Ireland
> - his life in the army.

Question (a) asks you to focus on Alexander and to consider one particular feature of his life – his isolation. Remember that you need to deliver a focused reponse that makes use of the bullet points.

> (b) **This question is about duty.**
>
> Show that the novel explores **differing kinds** of duty.
>
> In your answer, you should consider:
> - duty to parents
> - duty to country
> - anything else you think is relevant.

Question (b) asks you to focus on the **theme of duty** as it appears in the novel. Note that the question asks you to write about the topic more specifically, identifying and commenting on **differing kinds** of duty.

## How the examination question is structured

In framing a response, it is absolutely vital to identify the various requirements embedded in the terms of the question.

Look closely at Question (a) on *Of Mice and Men* in the 2006 Higher Tier paper:

(a) **This question is about Candy.**

Show how far you would agree that Candy is a **pitiable** character.

In your answer, you should consider:

- his hopes
- his fears
- his relationships with others.

Note the **key terms** of this question. The examiners always try to map out your response for you. Make sure you make use of the help they give you!

- The headline **identifies the character** the question is based on (**Candy**). You will need to say something about his relationships with other characters in the novel, but your focus must be firmly on how you view Candy – pitiable or otherwise.
- You are being invited to present **a sustained argument** and a **personal response**. You are required to 'show how far *you* would agree' that Candy is a pitiable character.

  *Note:* 'Show how far you would agree' is a very common lead-in to GCSE English Literature Prose text questions.
- The **focus of character evaluation** is in bold type – Candy as a '**pitiable** character'. You must focus on this aspect of his character.
- The implication is that you should consider the various ways in which the writer presents Candy as pitiable. In other words, you must consider **the writer's craft**.
- Bullet points act as a **guide to relevant areas of the novel** – 'in your answer you *should* consider ...'. If you ignore these instructions, you may be limiting the mark you can be awarded. If the examiner suggests you 'should do something', **do it**!

Similarly, look at Question (b) on *Of Mice and Men* in the 2006 Foundation Tier paper:

> (b) **This question is about loneliness.**
>
> Show that the novel is about the **loneliness of the ranch workers**. Which of them do you feel most sorry for? Give reasons for your opinions.
>
> In your answer, you should consider:
> - George
> - Candy
> - Crooks.

Again, make sure that you '**unpack**' the question carefully and respond to all the elements within it:

- The headline in bold **identifies the theme** on which the question is based – the loneliness of the ranch workers.
- You are invited to **form and develop an argument** ('Show that the novel is ...').
- This involves a **recognition of the writer's purpose** – commenting on what the novel is '**about**'.
- You are asked to give **personal response** ('Which of them do you feel most sorry for?').
- There is a requirement to back up your ideas with **textual reference** ('Give reasons for your opinions').
- The bullet points must be used; they are a guide to relevant areas of the novel. Again, if the examiner says you **'should'** consider these points, read that as '**must'**!

### Activity 4.9

In pairs, '**unpack**' the **key requirements in the following question**, making a logical list of bullet points, as in the two *Of Mice and Men* examples above. (This question is on *I'm the King of the Castle* by Susan Hill.)

(b) **This question is about Hooper.** *Foundation Tier*

Show that Hooper is both a **bully** and a **coward**. What do you think of him? Give reasons for your opinions.

In your answer, you should consider:
- what Hooper does to Kingshaw to show his power
- the things that frighten Hooper.

## Foundation Tier and Higher Tier questions

In a Foundation Tier question you are often given more guidance as to what to write about. For example, you might be given more precise directions as to the course of your essay.

Look at the difference between these Foundation and Higher Tier questions on *To Kill a Mockingbird:*

> (b) **This question is about family life.** *Foundation Tier*
>
> Show that the novel explores **loneliness and despair** in family life.
>
> In your answer, you should consider:
> - Boo Radley's home life
> - Mayella Ewell's relationship with her father
> - Maycomb's attitude to Boo and Mayella.

> (b) **This question is about family life.** *Higher Tier*
>
> Show how far you would agree that the novel explores **loneliness and desperation** in family life.
>
> In your answer, you should consider:
> - Boo Radley
> - Mayella Ewell
> - Dolphus Raymond
> - anything else you think is relevant.

Note the following points:

- The *stem* of the question is the same: the question is about '**family life**'.
- A more demanding argument is required by the Higher Tier question: '**Show how far would you agree that** the novel explores ...', rather than '**Show that** the novel explores ...'.
- The Foundation Tier bullet points give a more precise reference to the features of the text which you should be writing about, e.g. Boo Radley's '**home life**' rather than just generally 'Boo Radley'.
- The Higher Tier question asks candidates to consider a **third character**, Dolphus Raymond.
- The Higher Tier question invites the candidate, if necessary, to **range more widely** than the given characters, by mentioning 'anything else you think is relevant'.

Your tier of entry for the GCSE English Literature examination is a matter for you to decide carefully with your teacher.

## How to tackle the closed-book question

The Section B questions on prose texts are 'closed-book' questions. A 'closed-book' question means that you cannot take a copy of the textbook into the examination.

The special difficulties posed by the 'closed-book' question are that you:

- cannot check through the text to confirm your memory of events/characters
- cannot verify the **quotations** you may wish to use.

Therefore, in the examination you have to depend entirely on your own close knowledge and memory of the text and its various features. This means that a methodical programme of revision, with a review of all the notes that you have made about the text, is vital in the weeks/days leading up to the examination.

It may, however, be no bad thing that in the closed-book exam you do not have the temptation to waste time by flicking desperately through the text trying to find an event or a key phrase. Instead, you can focus on planning a coherent, relevant and convincing essay in response to the question set.

## Using quotations in a closed-book question

As in any English Literature exam, quotations should:

- be brief
- illustrate the point you are making
- be fluently embedded into your commentary.

It would be foolish to learn off by heart a large number of lengthy quotations for use in a closed-book examination, as there is more important revision work to be done! You are better off concentrating on memorising a number of short, key comments which will effectively illustrate the writer's intentions or his/her craft.

Here are some important tips for using quotations in a closed-book examination:

- Put **inverted commas** at the beginning and end of the quotation.
  Like all bullies, Hooper is a coward at the bottom and on more than one occasion Kingshaw sees him as a 'great blubbing baby'.
- Write the quotation **exactly as it appears in the original text.**
  'Four legs good, two legs better', **not** 'Four legs good but two legs are even better'.
- Do **not** use a quotation **simply to repeat a point** you have already made.
  Boxer is a hard-working animal. He says: 'I will work harder.' Instead, look at how this quotation could be integrated into an informed personal comment:

  Boxer's blind faith in sustained physical effort as the key to the success of Animalism is expressed in his often-repeated personal motto, 'I will work harder.'
- Use quotations to **illustrate** points you are making.
  Jack's savagery in the final conflict of the story is seen in the way he hurled his spear at Ralph, 'viciously, with full intention'.
- You can use a quotation **to make a point** (or points!) for you.
  George concisely sums up the main features of Lennie when he introduces him to Slim: 'Hell of a nice fella, but he ain't bright.'
- Make sure the quotation is **fluently embedded** into the sentence.
  Major Glendinning is a man who seldom shows compassion for his men. He has no sympathy with Private Crowe when he requests special leave to try to find his missing father but instead accuses him of simply looking for 'an easy billet'.
- Quotations should be **brief, meaningful** and **relevant**.
  Atticus does not condemn or demonize the men who come with the intention of lynching Tom Robinson; they are his neighbours and even though they are behaving like 'a gang of wild animals', he has the strong conviction that 'they're still human' underneath.

**Activity 4.10**

In groups, identify 4–6 key quotations in relation to the main characters in your novel.

- Explain to the rest of the class why your choices are significant.

These could form the bases of quotations you need to learn.

This exercise could usefully be repeated in relation to themes, setting and key moments in the text.

## Sample answers

This first sample answer is an essay on Steinbeck's *Of Mice and Men*.

Steinbeck: *Of Mice and Men* – this question is about the differing **kinds of power** that George, Lenny and Curley possess.

*George had the most control over Lennies life as Lennie wasn't right, so George was able to tell him what to do, were to go and most other things as well. Most of Lennies life was run by George because Lennie wasn't capable of doing it himself. George gets angry at times because he often has to get Lennie out of trouble, which Lennie cannot do himself – 'you do bad things and I got to get you out'. George was like a father type figure to Lennie. If anything was wrong or he needed anything at all he went to George or else if he was scared. So it was just like families, George was the father and Lennie was his son.*

*Even though Lennie wasn't able to do many things, his physical strength was unreal like the time they were living in Weed. Lennie saw a girl wearing a red dress, Lennie is the type of person that likes the feelings of things but he went over and started stroking this girl's dress, but he wouldn't let go and the girl started to get scared and started to screem. She then tried to acuse Lennie of raping her. So that's why they had to leave incase the people of Weed killed Lennie. There was another time that he wanted a puppy but he killed it just by stroking it because he was doing it to hard and the puppy was not long born. Then it got really bad when he killed Curly's wife when they were in the barn talking. Lennie started to stroke her hair but he wouldn't stop so Curley's wife started to panic and screamed. So Lennie put his hand over her mouth and lifted her and went to turn round but he was holding her so tight that as he spun around he broke her neck and killed her. So just because he couldn't look after himself didn't means he wasn't strong.*

*Curley had a very bad temper and took it out on the first person that annoyed him or else the first person he saw, even his wife. He lost his temper so bad one day that he broke his arm. He would even hit his own wife.*

Let's identify some of the **positive aspects** of the essay. The candidate has demonstrated:

- some knowledge of major events in the text, e.g the killing of Curley's wife
- some understanding of relationships, with the appropriate personal response that George was a 'father type figure' to Lennie
- the use of a relevant quotation to back up comment that George gets Lennie out of trouble
- some understanding of characters – the writer is aware that Curley 'had a very bad temper'
- an attempt to offer some response to all three bullet points.

However, there are obvious weaknesses as well. There is:

- a lack of specific textual reference in paragraph 1, no examples to illustrate how 'Lennie's life was run by George'
- an inclination to resort to narrative rather than commentary in paragraph 2 – simply retelling some events in the story is not presenting 'informed argument' (AO 1)
- lack of detailed development/illustration/commentary in paragraph 3
- limited awareness of the writer's use of language or prose techniques, etc (AO 2).

This second sample answer is an essay in response to a question on Harper Lee's *To Kill a Mockingbird*.

Lee: *To Kill a Mockingbird* – this question is about the presentation of **Atticus as a strong character**

*Atticus is a very strong and determined character in 'To Kill a Mockingbird'. Throughout the novel he has a sure confidence in his own beliefs and has the physical courage to stand up against injustice and prejudice. He is clearly the hero of the story.*

*We first see him when he is explaining to the children about their ancestry. He says they are both right about Simon Finch and this demonstrates that Atticus is always diplomatic and fair as he favours neither child's opinion. He is also a strong and influential figure because of his knowledge, as he is the person that the children naturally go to for information or advice. They refer to him as 'Atticus' and not as 'father' or 'dad'. In my opinion this reinforces their respect for him as a figure of wisdom and of power. He is not only the children's father, he is much more than that – he is their friend, their counsellor and their teacher.*

*At first Scout comments to Miss Maudie that Atticus was older than the fathers of their school friends and that he couldn't do impressive things, like run fast or shoot and that he didn't have an interesting job. Miss Maudie points out how wrong Scout is by revealing that he used to be called 'One-Shot Finch' and was 'the deadest shot in Maycomb county in his time'. We see that Atticus keeps this information from his children so as not to promote violence. This shows how he wants to bring up his children in a good way. It also shows that his strength is a quiet strength – he doesn't go around boasting about his shooting skill. It is his modesty that impresses here.*

*When Atticus takes on Tom Robinson's case, this demonstrates bravery and shows defiance of the citizens of Maycomb. He presents the defence case with self-confidence and composure and influences the jury so much that they are out for a long time considering their verdict. This shows that Atticus is bold enough to encourage change in the system of justice in Maycomb, despite the deeply-ingrained prejudice which has reigned there for so long. Even if it isn't a huge change or a resounding victory, Atticus is still an influential force on the prejudices of one town and this fact alone makes him a strong character. He is particularly strong and unshakable in his belief that 'in our courts all men are equal', no matter what their class or colour.*

*Atticus's presence in the town is felt by most people, especially because of his high profile in the Tom Robinson rape case. The ignorance and prejudice of the white townspeople inspire them to call him a 'nigger lover' and other names. Yet it is the black people, the second-class citizens, who recognise the powerful stand he is taking and commend him for it. It is also the insightful and truly good people such as Miss Maudie or Heck Tate who can see the good Atticus is doing. Here, Harper Lee inspires a feeling of admiration for Atticus as he is the champion of the underdog and does not fear being shunned for it.*

*Continued*

*Lee also uses the devices of his appearance, job and personality to demonstrate his strength. Atticus is a grey-haired, fifty year old lawyer, blind in one eye, certainly not the stereotypical hero. He is not a handsome and strapping heroic figure of masculinity, and so it is through his calm actions and his quiet, sure intelligence that we grow to love him. Lee also shows us Atticus through Scout's eyes. Through doing so, the reader is able to see why Scout says and does what she does, because her father is the predominant, inspirational figure in her life.*

*I find Atticus a truly inspirational character. He is a single parent but with the help of a well appointed maid and nurse he raises his children to become well-rounded, sensible and philosophical individuals. In terms of appearance and class he is nothing special, but it is his inspirational judgement calls, his words of wisdom, his patience and kindness and the quiet strength of his convictions that make him such an admirable character. In conclusion, I feel that Harper Lee very effectively presents Atticus as a character with both strength and a subtle intelligence.*

Let's identify the **positive aspects** of the essay. There is:

- the sense of a **well-constructed essay**, with confident and effective introduction and conclusion
- a strong **focus on the question**
- a clear, **confident personal response** offered – finds Atticus a 'truly inspirational character'
- an **assured interpretation of characters** – Atticus is 'champion of the underdog'
- an **evaluative response** – agrees he is a 'strong character', but argues that it is a quiet, modest strength
- a presentation of a **range of the character's strengths** – from shooting skills to moral courage
- an exploration of what a range of **other characters say and think** about him – his children, Miss Maudie, the white and the black people of the town
- some discussion of the writer's **narrative skills** – presenting Atticus 'through Scout's eyes'
- sustained, interesting and **fluent** argument
- a **persuasive**, **coherent answer** to the question set
- awareness of **'stereotypes' in literature** – Atticus is a different type of hero
- **quotation used to make the point** about his strong belief in the fairness of the courts.

This is an impressive response. It could have been improved by:

- including more reference to the writer's use of language
- incorporating more precise textual reference at times.

## Some practice questions

Here are practice questions on all of the prose texts specified for CCEA's GCSE English Literature examination. There is a Foundation Tier and a Higher Tier question in each case.

Have a go at the two questions on your text. Your teacher may help you with 'unpacking' the question and planning an appropriate answer. In Chapter 6 you will find a checklist of possible points for each of these questions.

## Johnston: *How Many Miles to Babylon?*

### Activity 4.11.1

*Foundation Tier*

**This question is about friendship.**

Show how the **friendship between Jerry and Alexander survives** in spite of all the difficulties. Give examples of the strength of their friendship.

In your answer, you should consider:

- the social and other differences between them
- how Alicia Moore and her husband tried to stop the friendship
- the difficulties of maintaining their friendship in the army.

### Activity 4.11.2

*Higher Tier*

**This question is about Major Glendinning.**

Show how far you would agree that Major Glendinning is **a character who can be both hated and admired**.

In your answer, you should consider:

- his harsh treatment of Alexander
- his strong sense of duty
- the way in which he led his men
- anything else you think is relevant.

## Orwell: *Animal Farm*

### Activity 4.12.1

*Foundation Tier*

**This question is about Squealer.**

Show that Squealer is the **most persuasive animal on the farm**. What are the main persuasive methods he uses? Give examples to back up your opinions.

In your answer, you should consider:

- how he changes the commandments
- the sort of information he gives to the rest of the animals
- how he defends Napoleon
- anything else you think is relevant.

### Activity 4.12.2
*Higher Tier*

**This question is about the abuse of power in the story.**

Show how far you would agree that the writer's purpose is **to show how easily power can be abused**.

In your answer, you should consider:

- the selfishness and greed of the pigs
- the exploitation of the 'lower animals', including Boxer
- Squealer's use of propaganda
- anything else you think is relevant.

## Lee: *To Kill a Mockingbird*

### Activity 4.13.1
*Foundation Tier*

**This question is about Atticus as a parent.**

Show how the writer presents Atticus as **a good parent for his children**. Do you think he was successful? Give reasons for your opinions.

In your answer, you should consider:

- what Jem and Scout think of their father
- how he tries to teach them good behaviour
- the example he sets them during his defence of Tom Robinson
- anything else you think is relevant.

### Activity 4.13.2
*Higher Tier*

**This question is about Scout.**

How far would you agree that the writer wants us to see Scout as **a character we should admire**?

In your answer, you should consider:

- her relationship with her brother Jem
- her relationship with her father
- her involvement in some of the events of the story
- anything else you think is relevant.

## Hill: *I'm the King of the Castle*

### Activity 4.14.1

*Foundation Tier*

**This question is about Hooper.**

Show how the writer presents Hooper as **the villain of the story**.

In your answer, you should consider:

- his bullying of Kingshaw
- how he lies to the adults
- his own cowardice at times
- anything else you think is relevant.

### Activity 4.14.2

*Higher Tier*

**This question is about the influence of setting on the behaviour of characters.**

Show how far you would agree that **the setting** Hooper and Kingshaw find themselves in has an influence on their behaviour?

In your answer, you should consider:

- life for Kingshaw and Hooper at Warings
- events in Hang Wood
- the trip to Leydell Castle
- anything else you think is relevant.

## Steinbeck: *Of Mice and Men*

### Activity 4.15.1

*Foundation Tier*

**This question is about violence in the novel.**

Show that the writer presents **different types of violence**. Which acts of violence do you think are the most shocking? Give reasons for your answer.

In your answer you should consider:

- the fight between Lennie and Curley
- the killing of Curley's wife
- the shooting of Lennie
- anything else you think is relevant.

### Activity 4.15.2

*Higher Tier*

**This question is about Lennie.**

Show how far you would agree that Lennie is a **character we should feel sorry for**.

In your answer, you should consider:

- his relationship with George
- how he is treated by Curley and Curley's wife
- his 'dream'
- anything else you think is relevant.

## Golding: *Lord of the Flies*

### Activity 4.16.1

*Foundation Tier*

**This question is about Piggy.**

At the end of the story Ralph wept for the loss of his 'true, **wise** friend called Piggy'. Show how Piggy is presented as **a wise and thoughtful character** who tried to help the other boys.

In your answer, you should consider:

- his concern for rules and organisation
- how he tried to help Ralph be a good leader
- how he tried to stand up against Jack and his savages.

### Activity 4.16.2

*Higher Tier*

**This question is about leadership.**

Show how far you would agree that **Ralph showed better leadership than Jack**.

In your answer, you should consider:

- Ralph's sense of responsibility
- Ralph's dependence on Piggy
- Jack's love of hunting and violence
- anything else you think is relevant.

# Chapter 5: *Poetry Anthology One*

## Sources of support for *Anthology One*

The advice, techniques and approaches that are discussed and exemplified in this chapter are equally relevant to the two anthologies prescribed in CCEA's English Literature specification. All the exemplification and essay questions in this chapter refer exclusively to *Anthology One* simply because it is the choice of virtually every centre taking this exam.

Before we begin work on the poetry section of this text, it is important that you are made aware that our material has been tailored to sit alongside CCEA's own award-winning web-based resource. This has been specifically designed to support pupils as they prepare to tackle the prescribed poetry anthologies in their GCSE English Literature examination.

This resource can be found at: www.rewardinglearning.com/poetryanthologies

Make sure you take maximum advantage of this website. Whether you want to sort your assonance from your alliteration, revisit individual poems, or gain further tips about answering questions, there is a wealth of useful information designed to provide you with stimulating and relevant pointers to develop your grasp of the poems in both anthologies.

The website presents:

- two different readings of each poem
- a detailed consideration of each, including:
  - information on each of the poets
  - individual summaries
  - points to ponder on
  - key features
  - the poems' impact
  - interpretations of the poems
- sample answers complete with commentaries
- writing tips to help you develop your answers
- a glossary of poetic terms which use examples drawn from the two anthologies.

On the website you can access much of the 'raw material' you will need to ensure that you have the required depth of knowledge to allow you to successfully complete this element of the exam. We have avoided bulking up this book by reproducing it, although some of the key pointers have been included for your benefit.

Other very useful resurces for working on Poetry Anthology 1 can be accessed at these CCEA websites:

www.rewardinglearning.com/development/qualifications/gcse/docs/support_materials/teacher_bookletcceaversion1.doc

www.rewardinglearning.com/development/qualifications/gcse/docs/support_materials/studentbookletCCEAversion.doc

## Key competences

Let's move on from resources to the practical business of readying ourselves to meet the challenge of this poetry anthology. There are a series of **key competences** that you need to have mastered in order to produce your best in the examination. Some of these will be developed through your studies in school or college; others will be a product of personal revision; and the remainder will be addressed in this chapter.

### Activity 5.1

Below are a series of questions. Your responses to them will act as a means of assessing your current exam-readiness and allow you to see what areas require your attention.

Have you:

- a sound knowledge of, and personal views about, the poems in the anthology you are studying?
- worked on the various themes and connections between the poems?
- an understanding of the specialist terms that you may need to write about poetry?
- an understanding of how to present quotations from poems?

Are you:

- aware of the particular styles of questions used to assess GCSE poetry?
- comfortable with the implications of the 'plain text' element of the exam?
- conscious of the 'compare-contrast' nature of this particular question and how you can best incorporate this into your answer?

It would be a surprise if at least some of these questions didn't create a degree of anxiety. By the time you have worked through the rest of this chapter, you should be able to answer these questions more positively and boost your confidence!

## Making efficient use of a plain text in the exam

How does a plain text impact on you, the candidate? This particular examining technique has advantages, but also disadvantages, as far as you are concerned:

1. The most positive feature from your perspective is that plain-text examining removes the need to become involved in the rote learning of chunks of text so that they can be regurgitated in the actual exam.
2. As you will have been issued with a copy of the anthologies, the written responses are expected to go beyond a simple demonstration of straightforward understanding. Access to a plain text gives candidates the freedom to focus on meaning, interpretation, poetic technique and language use.
3. Just because copies of the poems are provided does not mean that you don't have to develop that same close personal knowledge of the texts that

is required for Drama and Prose. Anyone who believes they can go into the exam, read the poems, then start to think about and analyse them prior to writing an answer will discover, to their cost, that this strategy doesn't work!

4 The copies of the poems are there:
   - for reference purposes
   - to allow you to include brief, precise quotations that support the point being made
   - to ensure that you can collate examples of, for instance, striking imagery; to contrast perhaps simple use of language with more complex constructions; or to allow you to illustrate precisely differing moods within or between poems.

5 *Remember*: the examiner will not give you *any* credit if you simply copy out large lumps of poems in an attempt to cover lots of sheets of paper!

## Technical terms in poetry

It's important that you are comfortable with and understand a range of the terms used to discuss poetry. If you want to see the range of technical poetic terms that you should understand, as well as examples from the poems you are studying, go to www.rewardinglearning.com/poetryanthologies/glossary

The primary object of learning about these terms is not just to be able to recognise a particular poetic feature within a poem. What is important is to recognise a particular feature in order to understand *what effect the poet is trying to achieve by using it*!

### Activity 5.2

In pairs, consider the following questions. They should help you to become more aware of and familiar with the poetic features used in *Anthology One* as well as helping you to focus on their purposes.

1 What effect is Gerard Manley Hopkins striving for with his use of repetition in 'All felled, felled, are all felled'?

2 List a series of metaphors that Hood uses to describe his boy (frequently to open a new stanza). How do they emphasise the innocent world of the small child?

3 For what purposes has Browning adopted the persona of the speaker in his poem?

4 Why does Shakespeare use natural imagery in 'Shall I Compare Thee to a Summer's Day?'

5 How does the sonnet form suit the purposes of Rossetti in 'Remember'?

6 Consider the effect of the reverse personification in the early stanzas of 'The Daffodils'.

7 How does Hardy use imagery in the opening stanzas to develop his view of the winter's evening?

8 How does Dickinson's use of imagery mirror the change in her attitude to the bird?

9 How does Bradstreet's type of language match her purpose?

## Presenting quotations appropriately in a plain text question

In a plain-text examination, you will be credited for using brief, appropriate quotations that precisely support the point being made. It would, therefore, be unusual to include quotes that go beyond a couple of lines.

Brief quotations, consisting of a word or phrase, can be embedded in the body of the essay. For example,

✓ Keats talks of 'plump the hazel shells' and 'a sweet kernel' ...

Quotations that are one complete line or longer would normally be presented in the following manner:

✓ Hardy cannot understand the reaction of the bird when he looks at the depressing surroundings they are sharing. There is:

> 'So little cause for carollings
>
> Of such ecstatic sound'

He has been depressed by the bleak winter's evening whereas the bird is 'ecstatic'.

It is perfectly acceptable to present this quotation in a more compact format, although this does tend to compress the writing and it isn't quite as easy on the examiner's eye. Generally, indenting longer quotations gives the work a more organised appearance.

Here is the last example presented using the compact style of format:

✓ Hardy cannot understand the reaction of the bird when he looks at the depressing surroundings that they are sharing. There is: 'So little cause for carollings/Of such ecstatic sound...' He has been depressed by the bleak winter's evening whereas the bird is 'ecstatic'.

## The 'dos and don'ts' of using quotations

Here are some examples from candidates that show you what to avoid when using quotations, and why. Having sorted out the pitfalls, we will consider how they can be put to good use.

### How not to use quotations

✗ ... if he comes home she will be happy. 'Then shall I celebrate thy praise, and bless for't even all my days.' She says that she will worship God for all her days if he brings her son back to her safely.

The candidate uses quotation without using either of the accepted presentational methods but, much more significantly, this excerpt falls into the trap of simply presenting a straightforward explanation of the quotation. This is another form of storytelling – what the Mark Scheme would describe as a 'simplistic comment'.

✗ Another method he uses to describe the beauty of autumn is the mention of its structure. 'With fruit the vines that round the thatch eaves run; To bend with apples the mossed cottage-trees.' Also he tells how the autumn matures the fruits ...

The candidate knows that he/she should be saying something about the poet's use of structure, but doesn't have a clear idea about it. He/she tries to cover this lack of understanding by quoting a couple of lines in an attempt to hoodwink the examiner into believing that it has something to do with 'structure'. *Don't attempt to write on something you know nothing about!*

✗ There is a simile at the beginning of The Daffodils – 'lonely as a cloud'.

Certainly this is a simile, but it's not enough to write out a piece of imagery and state that that's what it is. It's much more important to consider why the poet has included it. What effect/response does the poet hope to elicit from the reader? Don't rely on unsupported quotes to do your job - each one will need comment, analysis or explanation from you!

✗ Don't write a response to two poems without – at a series of points in your essay – quoting (words, phrases and/or lines) and commenting on the poets' choice and use of language to develop their views on the subject matter.

## Making effective use of quotations

✓ Keats develops his picture of autumn as one of 'ripeness to the core' through a series of verbs that capture his sense of the season's abundance – 'load', 'bend', 'fill', 'swell' and 'plump'.

Here the candidate is selecting appropriately, using a phrase and list of single words, to present concise analysis.

✓ The two poems also both use alliteration. Keats describes the 'wind' as 'winnowing' whilst Hardy describes his aged thrush as 'blast-beruffled'.

In this example, a candidate is using quotation as a tool to compare the poems. It would have been even more creditworthy had the different effects of these adjectives been contrasted: the long, languid, soft sound of 'winnowing' fitting in perfectly with Keats' luxurious view of autumn, while the harsh uncomfortable edge to 'blast-beruffled' exactly captures the feeling of Hardy's 'desolate' day.

✓ ... does not want to leave the beauty of autumn behind. In contrast to this Hardy describes everything as:

'... shrunken hard and dry,

And every spirit upon the earth

Seemed fervourless as I.'

He does not believe the season is beautiful but rather that it has sucked the life out of everyone, including himself.

There is a strong sense of purposeful comparison here. This is highlighted by the final comment that emphasises the difference in the attitude to the seasons that Keats and Hardy display.

## How to unpack the question

Before we actually begin our analysis of the questions, let's focus briefly on the important choices that have to be made in this section of the exam paper.

- The first of these choices has been made long ago - you studied one of the two anthologies and so naturally, you will select from the two questions on that anthology!
- Next, you have to choose from two possible questions - (a) or (b). Both of these questions require you to compare and contrast two poems that share a common theme.
- Question (a) requires you to compare and contrast the first specified poem with one of two other poems that are named in the question. The only element of choice is which of the two other named poems you choose.
- Question (b) specifies the first poem and the theme that you are to write about. The choice of the second poem is left up to you, but the choice must tie in with the specified theme!

We are going to look, first, at the form of the questions from *Anthology One* on the 2005 exam paper.

Both Foundation and Higher Tier papers use the same poems and themes; there is a common stem in both questions; the only difference is to be found in the form of the instructions to the candidates. These differences can be seen from the two annotated questions that follow.

**Question (a)**

The overall theme of the question is stated at the outset to ensure that the candidate is immediately made aware of the focus for the writing task.

A reminder of the focus of the question.

The candidate is asked to present his/her personal view on the poems.

**Question 12(a)** *Higher Tier*

**This question is about the seasons.**

Look again at 'To Autumn' by John Keats, and at **either** 'Shall I Compare Thee to a Summer's Day?' by William Shakespeare **or** 'The Darkling Thrush' by Thomas Hardy.

With close reference to the way the two poems are written, compare and contrast the way each poet conveys **the special qualities of the season**, and explain which poem appeals to you more.

It is this poem that will be compared and contrasted with one of the two poems that follow.

This is one of the most important instructions - compare and contrast **how** each poet presents his view. This tells the candidate to focus on the poets' use of language, form and the poetic techniques that each has used.

The overall theme of the question is stated at the outset to ensure that the candidate is immediately made aware of the focus for the writing task.

A reminder of the focus of the question.

The candidate is asked to present his/her personal view on the poems.

The examiner includes these three bullet points to give further guidance as to the areas you should consider in your answer.

**Question 12(a)** *Foundation Tier*

**This question is about the seasons.**

Look again at 'To Autumn' by John Keats, and at **either** 'Shall I Compare Thee to a Summer's Day?' by William Shakespeare **or** 'The Darkling Thrush' by Thomas Hardy.

From the way these two poems about the **seasons** are written, show how the poems are alike and how they are different, and explain which of the two poems you prefer.

In your answer, you should consider:

- what each poet has written about
- what you learn about the thoughts and feelings expressed in each poem
- anything else you think is relevant.

It is this poem that will be compared and contrasted with **one** of the two poems that follow.

The opening part of this instruction is central. It targets what the examiner wants you to focus on in your answer: the way the poems are 'written'. You are to compare and contrast the use of words and phrases and **how** the poets draw on various poetic techniques to develop their viewpoint.

**Question (b)**

In (b), the layout is similar to those described in detail above. The main difference is that the candidate has to choose the second, thematically-linked poem. Again, the stems in both papers are very similar and it is only at the point where the candidate is being instructed as to the focus of the answer that the papers are different.

**Question 12(b)** *Higher Tier*

**This question is about emotions for a loved one.**

Look again at 'A Parental Ode to My Son, Aged Three Years and Five Months' by Thomas Hood, in which the speaker conveys his mixture of emotions for his son, **and** at **one** other poem from the anthology in which the speaker conveys his or her mixture of emotions for a loved one.

With close reference to the way each writer has used language to convey the speaker's mixture of emotions, show which writer makes you feel more **sympathy** for the speaker.

Despite the slight difference in the wording, the instruction is the same – select a poem that fits in with the theme of 'emotion felt for a loved one'.

**Question 12(b)** *Foundation Tier*

**This question is about emotions for a loved one.**

Look again at 'A Parental Ode to My Son, Aged Three Years and Five Months', by Thomas Hood, in which the speaker conveys his mixture of emotions for his son. With reference to this **and** to **one** other poem from the anthology in which the speaker conveys his or her mixture of emotions for a loved one, show which speaker you feel more **sorry** for.

In your answer, you should:

- describe in your own words what each poem is about
- say what you learn about the thoughts and feelings of each speaker
- show how each poet uses language to convey these feelings.

Despite the slight difference in the wording, the instruction is the same – select a poem that fits in the theme of 'emotion felt for a loved one'.

This question offers more scope for the candidate to exercise a degree of personal choice. The Mark Scheme lists three poems that are likely to be paired with Thomas Hood's poem. If the choice goes beyond these three specified poems, the marker is told to 'be receptive to other relevant selections, which are carefully argued'. There is no reason to avoid tackling Question (b), but be very sure that, if you take it on, your choice is thematically relevant.

## Activity 5.3

On your own (because that's how you will be in the exam), see if you can come up with the three poems the examiner listed as the most likely to be selected.

*See Checklists on page 93.*

## How to deal effectively with the comparative element of the 'poetry' question

Having broken down the questions and their requirements, the next step is to select a means of meeting these demands.

Both of the questions will require you to **compare** and **contrast** two poems. The most effective way of accomplishing this is by creating a series of headings – these should be relevant to the question, common to both poems and provide you with a pathway through them.

The diagram below represents one way of going about this business. It is certainly not the only way, but it does offer a working model that can be adapted to the demands of a specific question. What actually goes into each of the four 'content' boxes around the central focus depends on the question you have to answer. This style of approach should ensure that you keep the focus of the question at the centre of the essay and also guarantee that you **'compare and contrast'** in a purposeful fashion throughout your answer.

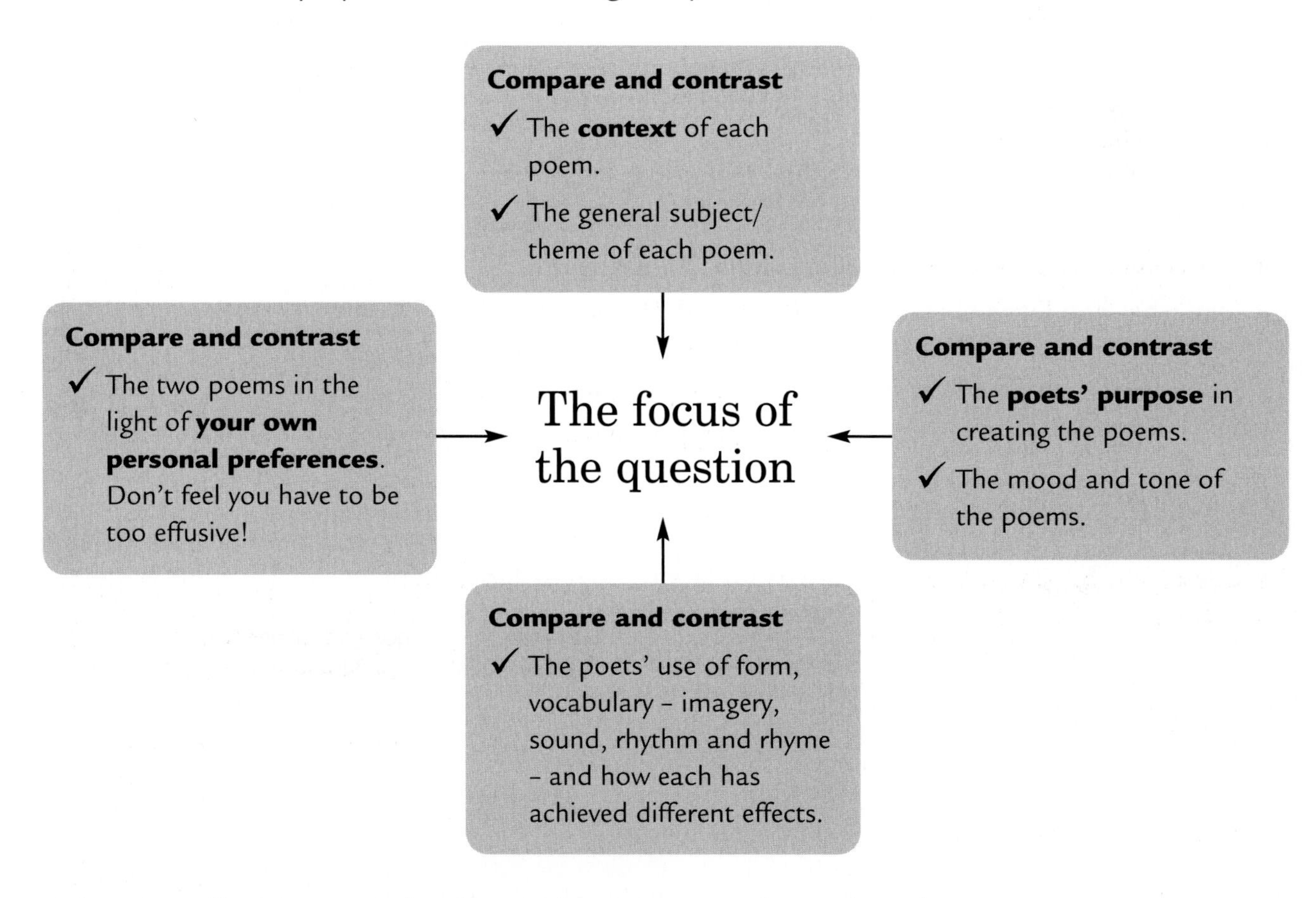


Below you will see an example of how this structure can be used to plan a relevant response to Question 12(b) (Higher Tier) on page 59.

(This plan is much more detailed than would be normally appropriate. This extra detail is included to demonstrate the type of points that could usefully be incorporated in such an answer.)

**Shared theme**

Both poems deal with love for a child.

Very different in approach – Hood shows his emotion in a perceptive, light-hearted manner that captures the roller-coaster ride of the proud father's emotions/Bradstreet's poem is an intense, personal plea to God for the safe return of her son who is about to undertake a perilous journey.

**Context**

Bradstreet's – seventeenth century; written in New England by Puritan mother; was frowned upon by male-dominated society – first American poet published. Hood was writing 150 years later – a London born editor and writer.

**Mixed emotions for a loved one HOW these are conveyed Bradstreet/Hood**

**Personal preference**

These poems are very different – Hood's work is memorable for its imagery and humour, whereas the impressive feature of Bradstreet's poem is the deeply personal and sincere feel of what is a mother's plea to God.

It's particularly refreshing to encounter a poem where humour is used, but that still has a serious message for its reader.

In the example essays that begin on page 66, the more successful response is obvious, because it focuses on the question and approaches the business of comparing and contrasting.

**Purpose**

Hood is highlighting for his reader the pride and delight of parenthood and at the same time humorously showing us the practicalities of rearing children – the less idealised reality of fatherhood.

Bradstreet, by contrast, shares with her reader the internal struggle she is suffering as her son prepares to set sail for England. She is demonstrating a different facet of parenthood – that sense of anxiety that every parent feels for their child's safety and welfare.

**Mood and tone**

Hood shares his parental pride and love with his reader whilst at the same time humorously reminding us of the less-than-ideal manner in which children behave.

Bradstreet is concerned at her son's impending journey. She is inevitably sad as well as hopeful of a safe outcome. The deeply personal pleading tone wavers as she finally entrusts her son to God's keeping.

**Use of form/vocab/imagery/rhythm and rhyme**

Hood's poem comprises six stanzas, each with their own rhyme scheme. Bradstreet's is twenty lines made up of rhyming couplets.

Bradstreet's language reflects the personal nature of her prayer – it's full of archaic words with religious overtones – 'celebrate thy praise'/'resign into thy hand'. Striking use of made-up word in final line 'happefy'd'.

Hood's work juxtaposes the idyllic with reality. Again the language is archaic but it is much lighter in feel and this is reflected in the form and composition of the poem. It has a series of metaphors describing the boy – 'Thou cherub but of earth'; similes – 'Light as the singing bird'; and alliteration, all used to emphasise the innocence of childhood.

# What the examiner is looking for – key indicators in the Mark Schemes

Not even examiners would claim that Mark Schemes are exciting documents! But they do let you know clearly what it is the examiner is looking for when you are asked a particular question. This means it is possible to tease out the significant elements that are always at the heart of a successful response – the key indicators you need to incorporate when writing an answer.

Assessment Objectives are at the centre of the examining process. This particular section of the exam is testing your ability to respond:

- critically, sensitively and in detail
- explore how language, structure and form contribute to the meanings of texts
- explore relationships and comparisons between texts, selecting and evaluating material.

These Assessment Objectives are developed into a series of task-specific points for each question. Below is an opportunity for you to take on the role of chief examiner!

## Activity 5.4

In groups, look again at Question 12(a) on page 57. Using your copy of *Anthology One*, apply your understanding of these poems to see if you can finish off each of the task-specific statements. They are quite straightforward!

John Keats

William Shakespeare

Thomas Hardy

**The scene or event which has affected each poet**

- Keats describes ...
- Shakespeare writes of ...
- Hardy describes ...

**General similarities and differences**

*The effect of the season on each poet:*

- Keats experiences ...
- Shakespeare contrasts ...
- Hardy is ...

*How the poets use changes in tone or sustain their tone in these poems:*

- Keats and Hardy ... , whereas Shakespeare ...

*The form of each poem:*

*Who or what each poet is addressing:*

- Keats addresses ...
- Shakespeare addresses ...
- Hardy's poem ...

*Each poet presents a different attitude:*

- Keats openly expresses ...
- Shakespeare expresses ...
- Hardy conveys how ...

*See Checklists on page 94.*

The other element of the marking process is the Assessment Matrix. This is a table that provides descriptions of stepped levels of performance for each of the AOs. Below is the Foundation Tier Poetry Assessment Matrix:

| **Assessment Objective** | **Band 1 Marks 0–10** | **Band 2 Marks 11–20** | **Band 3 Marks 21–30** | **Band 4 Marks 31–35** |
|---|---|---|---|---|
| **AO 1 Argument** | Some writing about text or task. | Simple, straightforward or limited response.<br>Attempt to focus on question.<br>Assertion, basic conclusion, narrative or description. | Begins to develop a response. / Fairly developed response.<br>Begins to focus on question. / Some focus on question.<br>Some argument. | Reasoned response.<br>Sustained focus on question. Developed argument. |
| **AO 2 Form and Language** | Simplistic comments about characters, setting and events.<br>Little awareness of structure, form or dramatic techniques. | Some awareness of significance of characters, setting and events.<br>Some awareness of structure, form or dramatic techniques.<br>Occasional reference to the writers' words. | Comments on characters, setting and events.<br>Comments on effects of structure, form or dramatic techniques.<br>Some understanding of the writers' use of language. | Interpretation of characters, setting and events.<br>Some discussion on the effects of structure, form or dramatic techniques.<br>Meaningful comment on some stylistic devices, with the emergence of a critical vocabulary. |
| **AO 3 Comparison and Contrast** | Poems considered in isolation. | Simple connections made between poems. | Attempt to explore obvious comparisons and contrasts between poems. | Recognition of, and response to, opportunities to compare and contrast poems. |

## How the examiner arrives at a final mark and what this means for you

Having read a response, the first thing the examiner does is match the characteristics of that essay with the Mark Band that most accurately matches the performance. The second step in the process is to decide exactly *where* within that Mark Band the essay fits. Is it just into that band, or is in the middle, or at the top?

If you are sitting the Foundation Tier, the descriptors in this table tell you a lot about what your essay should aim to do:

✓ offer a clearly **developed** and **organised** answer that answers the question in a **relevant** manner

✓ present some relevant comment on **the effect created by poetic form and technique** using some appropriate **critical terms**

✓ **compare and contrast** the poems **purposefully**.

The way to score heavily is clear:

- stay on task
- remember that form and technique play a major role in poetry, so comment on the effect that they have in developing the poets' meaning
- actively highlight contrasts and make comparisons.

This type of essay requires preparation, so you *must plan*!

Below is the Higher Tier Poetry Assessment Matrix. Studying it allows us to see what the examiner is looking for in a successful response.

| **Assessment Objective** | **Band 1 Marks 0–5** | **Band 2 Marks 6–15** | **Band 3 Marks 16–25** | | **Band 4 Marks 26–30** | **Band 5 Marks 31–35** |
|---|---|---|---|---|---|---|
| **AO 1 Argument** | Some writing about text or task. | Simple, straightforward or limited response.<br>Attempt to focus on question.<br>Assertion, basic conclusion, narrative or description. | Begins to develop a response.<br>Begins to focus on question.<br>Some argument. | Fairly developed response.<br>Some focus on question. | Reasoned response.<br>Sustained focus on question.<br>Developed argument. | Evaluative response.<br>Persuasive, coherent answer to the question.<br>Sustained argument. |

| Assessment Objective | Band 1 Marks 0–5 | Band 2 Marks 6–15 | Band 3 Marks 16–25 | Band 4 Marks 26–30 | Band 5 Marks 31–35 |
|---|---|---|---|---|---|
| **AO 2 Form and Language** | Simplistic comments about characters, setting and events. Little awareness of structure, form or dramatic techniques. | Some awareness of significance of characters, setting and events. Some awareness of structure, form or dramatic techniques. Occasional reference to the writers' words. | Comments on characters, setting and events. Comments on effects of structure, form or dramatic techniques. Some understanding of the writers' use of language. | Interpretation of characters, setting and events. Some discussion on the effects of structure, form or dramatic techniques. Meaningful comment on some stylistic devices, with the emergence of a critical vocabulary. | Assured interpretations of characters, setting and events. Developed discussion on the effects of structure, form or poetic techniques. Analysis of writers' language and style, using appropriate critical terminology. |
| **AO 3 Comparison and Contrast** | Poems considered in isolation. | Simple connections made between poems. | Attempt to explore obvious comparisons and contrasts between poems. | Recognition of, and response to, opportunities to compare and contrast poems. | A synthesised approach to detailed comparison and contrast. |

These descriptors have very clear implications for candidates sitting the Higher Tier. To score highly, an essay has to:

✓ maintain a **clearly developed focus** on the question

✓ use an **analytical approach**

✓ examine the ways the writers have employed **poetic structure and technique**, as well as offer an insight into **why** these have been used

✓ present a **confident interpretation**

✓ make use of **appropriate specialist terms** in the discussion

✓ **integrate comparison and contrast** throughout the essay.

This type of organised, analytical writing is achievable as a result of:

- thorough preparation throughout the course – there is no substitute for close knowledge and appreciation of the poems
- practice – if you are to be properly prepared, it is essential to use some of your revision time actually writing 50-minute essay answers
- making a plan – *before* writing your response in the examination!

## Sample answers

This first answer is a response to the Foundation Tier, Question 12(a). A copy of the task is to be found on page 58.

The opening does have some promise even if it is very straightforward. The problem is that the answer never develops any depth.

In common with many candidates, this person is confused as to the nature of the rhetorical question.

There is very clear reliance on repetition (see end of last paragraph). The lack of any significant use of quotation is another telltale sign of the general nature of the answer.

*The poems To Autumn by John Keats and Shall I Compare Thee to a Summer's Day? By William Shakespeare both share similaritys such as retorical questions and comparissons to nature. These two poems also have differences such as the lengths, the seasons and 'Shall I Compare Thee to a Summer's Day?' is a poem written to compare a person and there qualities to a Summers day, whereas A ode to Autumn is a poem which is describing the qualitys of Spring as it comes to an end.*

*Both these poems share similaritys, the first is that they both contain retorical questions in it such as 'Who hath not seen thee oft amid thy store?' Shall I Compare Thee to a Summer's Day? has one retorical question in it, which is also it's title. The two poems are also similar in that they both share the theme of nature and both talk about nature at certain seasons. Shakespeare's poem is about a typical Summers day and Keat's poem is about Springtime coming to an end.*

*These poems have differences such as there lengths. Shakepeare's poem is short and has one stanza long and Keat's is three stanzas long. The poems are also different as in Shakepeare's poem he is comparing a person to a Summers day. In Keat's poem he is talking about Springtime coming to an end.*

*I prefer Shakepeare's poem as it is short, to the point and it is a poem of positiveness and it is a very beautiful poem, in the way he is complamenting this person.*

The use of 'spring' could be overlooked as a one-off error – a sign of a candidate under pressure – if it weren't for its general use throughout the whole piece!

This discussion clearly demonstrates the candidate's lack of basic understanding.

Still attempting to answer relevantly, but lack of detailed understanding inevitably leads to another simple, generalised comment.

A straightforward response.

Simple connections made between poems.

Basic conclusions.

### Activity 5.5

*Foundation Tier*

The candidate understands what is required by the question but simply doesn't have sufficiently detailed knowledge to produce more than an extremely superficial response.

Take 30 minutes and 'overhaul' this essay. Develop the few points it makes and include relevant quotations to turn it into a more detailed and appropriate response.
*See Checklists on page 94.*


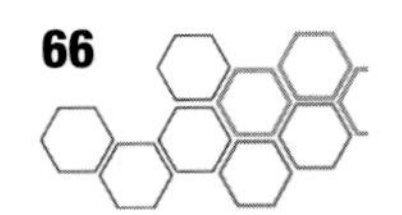

This is a response to Question 12(a) of the Higher Tier examination. A copy of the task is to be found on page 57.

*'To Autumn' written by John Keats is a poem expressing his admiration and love for the season Autumn. This poem is made up of 3 stanzas and each line contains 10 syllables. Keats has chosen this form so that he can illustrate his change of emotion as the season of Autumn passes.*

> Later in the essay, this sense of a 'change' is contradicted. Suggests a failing in planning.

*The tone of 'To Autumn' is one of appreciation and excitement shown in the opening line 'Season of mists and mellow fruitfulness'. He has created the tone from the very start of the poem. He has used punctuation to express excitement and words such as 'sweet', 'ripeness' and 'bless' to reinforce his positive attitude towards the season.*

> Inappropriate word selection

> Effective use of embedded quotes.

*On the other hand Shakespeare compares his love to the season Summer. He explains that summer is not as perfect as his lover who is 'more lovely and more temperate'.*

> Effective use of appropriate contrasting connective.

*The tone of 'Shall I Compare Thee to a Summer's Day' is one of happiness, but Shakespeare points out the disadvantages of summer, 'Rough winds do shake the buds of May.'*

*Shakespeare has chosen to write in the form which many poets chose to write about love in 1601. His language is exaggerated and romantic as poets in those days thought of true love to be perfect and romantic.*

> It's unfortunate that the writer has forgotten/ didn't know the form was a sonnet.

*Keats has used a rhythm and rhyme which stay constant throughout the poem. He has done this so that the reader can relax while reading the poem. The constant rhythm and rhyme allow Keats to express his joy without startling the audience. The rhythm and rhyme effect the mood of the poem and Keats has kept these the same so there is no tonal or mood shift.*

> There is a less assured, more general feel to the comments in this and the next paragraph.

> Not as suggested in the first paragraph.

*Shakespeare has also kept a constant rhythm and rhyme scheme which allows him to keep the mood of the poem the same.*

*Both poets have used similar rhythm and rhyme to allow them to address their favourite parts of each season without surprising the reader.*

> Some general comparisons drawn.

*Continued*

In the next two paragraphs the writer is once more competently responding and showing a more thorough grasp.

*Imagery is the main form in which both poets illustrate the special qualities about their season. Keats uses phrases such as 'the last oozing hours by hours.' He has used onomatapoeia to make the season seem to last long. He also points out disadvantages of summer to make his chosen month seem more beautiful and interesting. He does this when he says, 'Summer has o're brimmed their clammy cells.' Keats has used negative language, the word 'clammy', and associated it with summer. Descriptive language such as 'ripeness to the core' gives the reader a vivid picture as to 'what the poet is talking about. The word 'ripeness' tells the reader that every single part of the fruit is ripe.*

*Shakespeare also uses discriptive language to emphasize special qualities of the season. 'Sometime to hot the eye of heaven shines.' A metaphor like this comparing the sun to the 'eye of heaven' lets the target audience know the special way Shakespeare sees parts of summer. Shakespeare also says that the negative point of summer is that it 'hath too short a date.' By putting this line in simple straight forward language Shakespeare has highlighted that he thinks this is the worst thing about summer.*

Attempts to conclude with an evaluative comparison – some success.

*Both poets have used similar methods, similar exaggerated description and structure to the poem, to convey special parts of Autumn more clearly than Shakespeare describing summer. Shakespeare's tonal shift at the end of his poem, turning to arrogance by saying 'so long lives this and gives life to thee,' has made me prefer 'To Autumn' as it has not changed tone throughout and the poet simply states how he feels about Autumn.*

The conclusion with its personal preference is not the strongest feature of the answer.

Fairly developed – some focus on question.

Some understanding of use of language.

Comparative style throughout.

**Activity 5.6** *Higher Tier*

You can see that with a more thorough understanding of the function of rhyme and rhythm, this candidate could have produced an even better essay. In groups, discuss what the candidate could have usefully written to improve paragraphs 6 and 7.

On your own, and in 20 minutes, 'overhaul' these two paragraphs and improve the rather weak concluding paragraph.

**Activity 5.7**

Using the guidance in the Assessment Matrix for this task (page 74), assess and mark the revised answer produced by another pupil in your class. Offer a summary of the strengths of their answer, as well as selecting the Mark Band and score awarded. Now justify your marks!

# Practical preparation

## Themes in *Anthology One*

What follows is a list of *possible* themes. It is *probable* that the examiner will come up with different associations, so be prepared to think about and make important connections between poems in the examination. It is all part of the planning process!

Several of these poems fit into more than one theme, so they appear more than once.

**The seasons**
'The Darkling Thrush'
'Ode to Autumn'
'Shall I Compare Thee to a Summer's Day?'

**Loss of love**
'Break, Break, Break'
'Remembrance'
'Remember'

**Poems in the first person**
'My Last Duchess'
'The Burial of Sir John Moore'
'A Parental Ode'

**Place**
'Binsey Poplars'
'The Darkling Thrush'
'The Daffodils'
'Break, Break, Break'
'On the Tombs of Westminster Abbey'

**Death**
'Death the Leveller'
'On the Tombs of Westminster Abbey'
'The Burial of Sir John Moore'
'Break, Break, Break'

**Love**
'Upon My Son Samuel His Going for England, November 6, 1657'
'My Last Duchess'
'Shall I Compare Thee to a Summer's Day?'
'A Parental Ode'

**Poems of contrasting mood and emotion**
'A Parental Ode'/'My Last Duchess'
'Daffodils'/'Darkling Thrush'
'The Burial of Sir John Moore'/'Break, Break, Break'

**Loss**
'Break, Break, Break'
'Binsey Poplars'
'Remembrance'

**Joy and delight**
'A Parental Ode'
'The Daffodils'
'Ode to Autumn'

# Some practice questions

To give you a chance to practise, here some sample questions. You must get used to working at 'exam speed' – writing an essay in 50 minutes. It is also essential that you employ the timescales discussed in Chapter 2, so you get used to the thinking–planning–writing–revising process. In Chapter 6 you will find a checklist of possible points for each of these questions.

## Activity 5.8.1

*Higher Tier*

Question 12(a)

**This question is about place.**

Look again at 'Binsey Poplars' by Gerard Manley Hopkins, and at **either** 'The Daffodils' by William Wordsworth **or** 'On the Tombs of Westminster Abbey' by Francis Beaumont.

With close reference to the way the two poems are written, compare and contrast the way each poet conveys **the special qualities of the place**, and explain which poem appeals to you more.

## Activity 5.8.2

*Foundation Tier*

Question 12(a)

**This question is about place.**

Look again at 'Binsey Poplars' by Gerard Manley Hopkins, and at **either** 'The Daffodils' by William Wordsworth **or** 'On the Tombs of Westminster Abbey' by Francis Beaumont.

From the way these two poems about places are written, show how the poems are alike and how they are different, and explain which of the two poems you prefer.

In your answer, you should consider:

- what each poet has written about
- what you learn about the thoughts and feelings expressed in each poem
- anything else you think is relevant.

## Activity 5.9.1

*Foundation Tier*

Question 12(b)

**This question is about love.**

Look again at 'Upon My Son Samuel his Going for England, November 6, 1657' by Ann Bradstreet, in which the speaker conveys her emotions for her son. Write about this **and one** other poem from the anthology in which the speaker conveys his/her love.

With close reference to the way each writer has used language to convey the speaker's love, show which writer creates more intensity of emotion.
*See possible plan for this essay on page 61.*

## Activity 5.9.2

*Foundation Tier*

Question 12(b)

**This question is about love.**

Look again at 'Upon My Son Samuel his Going for England, November 6, 1657' by Ann Bradstreet, in which the speaker conveys her emotions for her son. Write about this **and one** other poem from the anthology in which the speaker conveys his or her love. Explain which poem you prefer.

In your answer, you should:

- describe in your own words what each poem is about
- say what you learn about the thoughts and feelings of each speaker
- show how each poet uses language to convey these feelings.

*See possible plan for this essay on page 61.*

## Activity 5.10.1

*Higher Tier*

Question 12(a)

**This question is about unexpected encounters.**

Look again at 'A Bird Came Down the Walk' by Emily Dickinson, and at **either** 'The Daffodils' by William Wordsworth **or** 'The Darkling Thrush' by Thomas Hardy.

With close reference to the way the two poems are written, compare and contrast the way each poet conveys **the special qualities of the encounter**, and explain which poem appeals to you more.

## Activity 5.10.2

*Foundation Tier*

Question 12(a)

**This question is about unexpected meetings.**

Look again at 'A Bird Came Down the Walk' by Emily Dickinson, and at **either** 'The Daffodils' by William Wordsworth **or** 'The Darkling Thrush' by Thomas Hardy.

From the way these two poems about meetings are written, show how the poems are alike and how they are different, and explain which of the two poems you prefer.

In your answer, you should consider:

- what each poet has written about
- what you learn about the thoughts and feelings expressed in each poem
- anything else you think is relevant.

### Activity 5.11.1

*Higher Tier*

Question 12(b)

**This question is about sorrow and loss.**

Look again at 'Remember' by Christina Rossetti, in which the speaker conveys her emotions. Write about this **and one** other poem from anthology in which the speaker conveys his or her sense of sorrow and loss.

With close reference to the way each writer has used language to convey the speaker's sense of sorrow and loss, show which writer makes you feel more sympathetic for the speaker.

### Activity 5.11.2

*Foundation Tier*

Question 12(b)

**This question is about sorrow and loss.**

Look again at 'Remember' by Christina Rossetti, in which the speaker conveys her emotions. Write about this **and one** other poem from the anthology in which the speaker conveys his or her feelings of sorrow and loss. Explain which poem you prefer.

In your answer, you should:

- describe in your own words what each poem is about
- say what you learn about the thoughts and feelings of each speaker
- show how each poet uses language to convey these feelings.

# Chapter 6: Checklists

Where it was felt to be useful, we have included pointers that should be constructive. Bear in mind that with English Literature there is always room for differing interpretations, so don't become too caught up in the 'answers' we've provided.

## Chapter 2: Effective essay writing

### Page 4: **Activity 2.1**

Below is a list of the main features that would go to make up an effective essay:

- a sustained, relevant focus on the question
- a response that clearly demonstrates an organised, structured progression through the various elements of the question
- a close understanding of the text or texts that enables the candidate to display breadth and depth of knowledge
- analysis and exemplification that is concise and avoids unnecessarily lengthy explanation, over-elaboration or vagueness.

### Page 6: **Activity 2.2**

Below are a few pointers as to possible areas for improvement and as well as suggestions about trimming down some elements of the answer:

- The paragraph on George really doesn't get to the heart of George's 'power'– his genuine care and Lennie's absolute trust in him. This needed further development.
- The comparatively lengthy paragraph on Lennie spends too much time highlighting examples of Lennie's power rather than putting the character's physical power in its context – he is 'powerless' without George. This section of the essay could have been shortened to allow for greater development of the paragraphs on the other two characters.
- The discussion of Curley recognises his weakness and insecurity, but rather strangely attributes this to the notion that no one else liked him.
- The answer concludes with the personal perspective that is invited by the question – a more fluent expression of the final point would have rounded off the answer more effectively.

### Page 6: **Activity 2.3**

Possible alterations:

- Extend and improve the introduction.
- Too many 'Lennies' in second paragraph – change phrasing.
- The following sentence doesn't really capture the sense of what the candidate was trying to express and could benefit from revising:
  Lennie uses this uncontrolable [sp.] physical strength again in the killing of the puppy and Curley's wife.
- In the same paragraph, the sentence beginning 'A similar incident happened ...' is too long – turn into two sentences.

### Page 11: **Activity 2.7**

This opening contains a couple of valid, if unsupported points. They would form the basis of a reasonable introduction IF they were expressed more fluently. Below is a more precise expression of the points the writer made:

Initially, Alexander is shown to have a sensitive nature. As the events of the novel unfold, he matures and becomes tougher, although he manages to retain that sensitive, caring element within his character.

## Page 11: **Activity 2.8**

Once again, remember this is not definitively correct – just a suggestion.

This is competent writing. It is focused on task and analytical, making good use of relevant quotation and appropriate examples. Below are a couple of minor alterations that could further improve the piece:

- To be grammatically correct, 'suggests' on the first line should be 'suggest'.
- Too many 'suggests' and 'suggesting' in close proximity.
- The third sentence doesn't quite explain the sense of his feeling 'better than others'.

The following Assessment Matrix is to be used, along with the question-specific checklist, in order to assess the answers written in response to the sample questions in Chapters 3, 4 and 5.

| **Assessment Objective** | **Higher Band 1 Marks 0–5** | **Higher Band 2 Marks 6–15** | **Higher Band 3 Marks 16–25** | **Higher Band 4 Marks 26–30** | **Higher Band 5 Marks 31–35** |
|---|---|---|---|---|---|
| | Found. Band 1<br>Marks 0–10 | Found. Band 2<br>Marks 11–20 | Found. Band 3<br>Marks 21–30 | Found. Band 4<br>Marks 31–35 | |
| **AO 1 Argument** | Some writing about text or task. | Simple, straightforward or limited response.<br>Attempt to focus on question.<br>Assertion, basic conclusion, narrative or description. | Begins to develop a response. / Fairly developed response.<br>Begins to focus on question. / Some focus on question.<br>Some argument. | Reasoned response.<br>Sustained focus on question.<br>Developed argument. | Evaluative response.<br>Persuasive, coherent answer to the question.<br>Sustained argument. |
| **AO 2 Form and Language** | Simplistic comments about characters, setting and events.<br>Little awareness of structure, form or dramatic techniques. | Some awareness of significance of characters, setting and events.<br>Some awareness of structure, form or dramatic techniques.<br>Occasional reference to the writers' words. | Comments on characters, setting and events.<br>Comments on effects of structure, form or dramatic techniques.<br>Some understanding of the writers' use of language. | Interpretation of characters, setting and events.<br>Some discussion on the effects of structure, form or dramatic techniques.<br>Meaningful comment on some stylistic devices, with the emergence of a critical vocabulary. | Assured interpretations of characters, setting and events.<br>Developed discussion on the effects of structure, form or poetic techniques.<br>Analysis of writers' language and style, using appropriate critical terminology. |
| **(POETRY ONLY)**<br>**AO 3 Comparison and Contrast** | Poems considered in isolation. | Simple connections made between poems. | Attempt to explore obvious comparisons and contrasts between poems. | Recognition of and response to opportunities to compare and contrast poems. | A synthesised approach to detailed comparison and contrast. |

# Chapter 3: The drama section

Assess your answer using the following individual checklists for each question, along with the Assessment Matrix on page 74.

**In your essay there must be clear evidence that you have addressed the stem of the question.**

## Page 26: **Activity 3.10.1**

Wilder: *Our Town*

*Higher Tier* **Question about the Stage Manager**

The following textual details may be used to answer the question:

*How he controls time:*

In the extract:

- immediately engages with time change: 'This time nine years have gone by, friends – summer 1913' – clarifies the year, the season and the lapse in time from the beginning of Act 2
- uses the dates on the gravestones to emphasise the theme of death and the passing of time in an historical sense
- mentions historical events: 'Daughters of the American Revolution'/ 'Mayflower'/'Civil War veterans' – connects with time/significant events in the relatively short but chequered history of the U.S.
- passing of time in the universal sense – again emphasises moving from the personal/local to national to humanity as a whole: 'everybody knows ... every human being' – reflects key theme of universal versus particular.

In the play as a whole:

Act 1

- establishes date as well as precise geographical location amongst many other detailed particulars at beginning of this act
- time allowed to be fluid/omnipotent character sees past, present and future: 'First automobile's goin' to come along in about five years'
- refers to cemetery tombstones and the earliest date/comes full circle in Act 3
- precise about the time of day: 'just before morning'/'early morning'
- Mr and Mrs Gibbs are introduced and their time of death is outlined as well as legacy of the hospital Mr Gibbs left.

Act 2

- begins by stating: 'Three years have gone by ... thousand days'
- makes detailed reference to the huge earthly/universal changes that have occurred and the local/human developments
- then pinpoints time: 'It's 1904. It's July 7th ...'
- (His control of time has probably 'limitless' possibilities, e.g. announces time at end of play as if only one day has passed.)

*How he interacts with the audience:*

In the extract:

- addresses them directly at the beginning of this act and each subsequent act
- is their main source of information: details time/geographical historical and social changes
- creates a personal connection between the audience and the characters so we too feel sense of loss/gives us information to jog our memories and so deepen connection felt: 'There's your friend Mrs Gibbs ... the wedding so much, remember?'
- introduces characters, ideas and important themes: 'there's Joe Stoddard'/ 'There's something way down deep that's eternal about every human being'.

In the play as a whole:

- he is the authority on everything in the play
- creates a visual image of what is possibly a minimalist stage: 'Here's a couple of trellises for those who have to have scenery'/'This is Mrs Gibbs' garden'
- firmly presents play as a piece of theatre by introducing Producer and actors
- describes each character: 'In our town (one of many references to the title) we like to know the facts about everybody'
- interrupts action to update audience: 'I want to tell you something about that boy Joe Crowell ...'
- closes and opens each act: 'That's the end of the First Act, friends. You can go out and smoke now, those that smoke'
- uses the introduction to each act to update audience on the time passed.

*How he interacts with the other characters:*

In the extract:

- introduces the characters to the audience
- watches their interactions.

In the play as a whole:

- interacts directly with characters as audience members/a device to show Wilder's awareness of concerns at the time: Woman in the Balcony – her question draws attention to Simon Stimson's drinking; Man in the Auditorium – who the Stage Manager demands to 'Come forward' asks 'Is there no one in town aware of social injustice ...?'; Lady in the Box – used to answer Wilder's critics that this play lacked literary value: 'we've got a lot of pleasures of a kind here'. Wilder suggesting that this woman (and therefore his critics) missed the point of his play, i.e. to appreciate the simple pleasures of life
- takes a key role in Emily and George's courtship and marriage, a relationship which forms the backbone of the play/takes on the role of Mr Morgan during their heart to heart/removes the baseball players from the stage (an obstacle to the relationship)/acts as the Minister
- key interaction with the 'dead' Emily who asks him 'But it's true isn't it? I can go and live, back there – again'/Emily's return to 'an important day' used to drive home key themes/Stage Manager 'directs' this entire scene.

*Now use the relevant section of the Assessment Matrix on page 74 to score your essay.*

## Page 27: **Activity 3.10.2**

Wilder: *Our Town*

*Foundation Tier* **Question about love**

The following textual details may be used to answer the question:

*George and Emily's feelings for each other in the extract:*

- love demonstrated by George's recognition that Emily's criticism actually suggests her feelings for him: 'I'm glad you spoke to me about that – that fault in my character'
- Emily declares her love without actually saying the words: 'I – I am now; and I always have been'
- George's innocent realisation: 'So I guess this is an important talk we've been having'
- moves to the wedding and the birth of a baby – feelings develop into the everlasting through a tragically short-lived marriage.

*Wilder's use of stage directions and dramatic techniques in the extract:*

- the young lovers are looking for confirmation that the other feels the same way: *(She looks at him wide-eyed, he at her)* – suggests first moment of innocent truth
- Emily is reduced to being *(joyously tearful)* and George too *(almost weeping)* – stage directions used to emphasise the significance of the conversation
- creates their embarrassment and discomfort at the magnitude of the discussion they are having/emphasises how young and innocent they are/how unused to articulating their feelings: *(Almost pleadingly)*; *(terribly embarrassed)*; *(Squirming)*



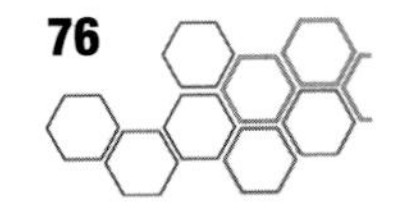

- stage directions throughout this extract (and the play as a whole) suggest Wilder's authority within the play – he has very clear ideas about how the play should be staged and what messages he wanted to convey about love and other issues.

*The importance of family life in Act 1:*

- establishes the two key, neighbouring families in the play – the focus of the romance/key characters
- introduces the theme of Death: 'Doc Gibbs died in 1930 ... Mrs Gibbs died first long time ago'/we return to cemetery at end of play when Mrs Gibbs and Emily are related through marriage/the marriage unites the two families
- introduces the birth of the twins/cycle of life is a key theme/ends for Emily at end of Act 3 when she dies in childbirth
- establishes marriage/affection between Mr and Mrs Gibbs: 'I do wish you could go away some place and take a rest'
- the discipline of both mothers in getting their children ready for school/the love, time and affection they have given to their children: When Mrs Gibbs said, 'I washed and ironed the blue gingham for you special', Rebecca replied, 'Oh Ma, I hate that dress'/by end of play, Emily, witnessing her own life, realises that these small things come to be the most significant
- the crossover of conversation between the two households establishes breakfast and mother/children relationships as universal
- sibling rivalry between George and Rebecca/Emily and Wally is something to which the audience can relate.

*How important it is to love life in Act 3:*

- Mrs Soames comments, after Mrs Gibbs tells her that Emily has died in childbirth: 'My, wasn't life awful – and wonderful'/childbirth, as Emily herself illustrates, combines both pain and the miracle of life
- Mrs Soames also reflects on the accomplishments in Emily's life
- Emily suggests, 'Live people don't understand, do they?' – this line introduces a key idea within this act
- Emily wants to return/warned against it by both Mrs Gibbs and Mrs Soames/chooses her 12th birthday/becomes 'an audience' in her own life/realises she has forgotten small but significant details/'passionately' addresses her mother: 'Just look at me as if you really saw me'/tells her about all about her marriage, baby and death/finds out the trouble people went to for her birthday
- Emily says goodbye to each significant thing and the small things that make life: 'Good-bye to clocks ticking ... hot baths'/'Oh Earth, you're too wonderful for anyone to realise you!'
- Act 3 suggests that it is important to love life, to embrace all its huge offerings because life is such a fleeting thing.

*Now use the relevant section of the Assessment Matrix on page 74 to score your essay.*

## Page 27: **Activity 3.11.1**

Russell: *Blood Brothers*

*Higher Tier* **Question about parenthood**

The following textual details may be used to answer the question:

*What the two women say and how they behave in the extract:*

- fact that the welfare have intervened suggests situation is out of control
- 'I love the bones of every one of them' – the key to being a good parent is loving your children – but Mrs Johnstone also realises 'kids can't live on love alone'
- Mrs Lyons rapidly seizes the opportunity: 'give one to me' – creates the story of the possible miscarriage for her husband
- Mrs Lyons uses Mrs Johnstone's weaknesses against her – manipulative – we judge her as a person and as a woman/mother
- Mrs Johnstone feels sorry for her: 'Are y' that desperate to have a baby?' – this instant affection makes her a good mother

- the writer creates sympathy for Mrs Lyons by detailing her dream about having a baby – does wanting something so much mean she will be a good mother when she gets what she wants?
- we realise that from a material sense Mrs Lyons can provide everything Mrs Johnstone can't. The two families/class situations are put into immediate contrast – materially one has everything; the other nothing at all.

*What you learn elsewhere in Act 1 about how Mrs Johnstone brings up her family:*

- had to get married
- had seven children and another pregnancy by the age of 25 – obviously likes babies/wanted a large family but was this irresponsible?
- can't afford to pay for basic necessities like milk
- kids long for simple things: milk for the baby; not to be on 'free dinners'; food to eat. Mrs Johnstone wishes she could provide more for them – do we judge her for having children she can't afford to look after or do we feel sorry for her situation as an abandoned mother who does her best and works hard as a cleaner to keep her family together under very difficult circumstances?
- do we judge her for her catalogue shopping or sympathise with her? The Catalogue Man and Finance Man both offer judgements
- she lies to her children about where 'the other twinny' went. This deals with the key question – do we think Mrs Johnstone was right or wrong to give up Edward?
- seven years on she's still avoiding the rent man – she is unable to escape the financial hardship of her situation: 'Did you think I was the rent man?'
- when Mickey and Edward meet we are immediately aware of the huge differences in their lifestyles – accent/language/education
- do we judge Mrs Johnstone for Sammy's head injury?
- do we judge her for the policeman's indication of previous crimes – of Sammy. Does this change when we witness how the policeman treats the same crime at the Lyons' home?
- Mrs Johnstone's delight at getting a new start – highly indicative of her desire to escape her current situation/wish for a better future for her family.

*What you learn elsewhere in the play about the relationship between Mrs Lyons and Edward:*

- overprotective towards Edward – overreacts to his meeting with Mickey/demonstrated further when she 'hits Edward hard and instinctively'/her move to then 'cradling him' and calling him 'my beautiful, beautiful son' shows her mental instability and it's this that complicates our judgement of her as a parent
- she overreacts to Edward 'bunking under the fence' but we can feel sorry for her (apart from financially) – e.g. Mr Lyons is as absent as Mr Johnstone and this creates sympathy for her/does this intensity of love make her a good parent?
- the dancing between Edward and his mother suggests a closeness in their relationship. (Previous to this scene, however, we are reminded that Mrs Johnstone still thinks about Eddie: she still loves him even though he is no longer a part of her life – the act of a true mother?)
- Edward is aware of his mother's instability: 'Are you feeling all right Mummy? You're not ill again ...?'

*Who is to blame for the twins' death and anything else you think is relevant.*

- Linda and Edward: for having an affair/for their betrayal of Mickey
- Mickey: for his dependency on pills/not listening to Linda who tries to help him and making the affair inevitable/for pulling the trigger
- Mrs Lyons: for tricking Mrs Johnstone into giving up her baby/for telling Mickey about the affair
- Mrs Johnstone: for tempting fate and superstition by separating the twins/her weakness in allowing Mrs Lyons to coerce her
- or is it, as the writer/Narrator suggests, the class system and the spectre of unemployment which lets the Johnstone family down.

*Now use the relevant section of the Assessment Matrix on page 74 to score your essay.*

## Page 28: **Activity 3.11.2**

Russell: *Blood Brothers*

*Foundation Tier* **Question about Mickey and Edward's friendship**

The following textual details may be used to answer the question:

*What they say and do when they first meet in the extract:*

- contrasted by their demeanour/language/accent/dialect/education
- Edward is 'bright and forthcoming'; Mickey is 'suspicious' – suggests he is less innocent/more streetwise than the generous Edward
- their financial situation is contrasted by the sweets – Edward has enough to share
- Edward is immediately delighted by Mickey's stories and language: 'Oh, that sounds like super fun'/'You say smashing things don't you' – suggests he's lonely for company and Mickey finally has someone he can boss around
- Edward's loneliness is emphasised further by his desire to be Mickey's best friend/the simplicity of their relationship is poignant at this point
- the mutual shedding of their blood in the 'Blood Brothers' ceremony prophesises/ foreshadows the bloodshed that is to come at the end of the play.

*How their friendship builds up in Act 1:*

- Mrs Lyons feels the need to intervene (again foretells what's to come in the future), as does Mrs Johnstone, in an attempt to prevent the inevitable from happening
- Linda is introduced as another factor in the relationship between them – one who will become increasingly important
- scene with the policeman (again foretelling of tragic end)
- when Edward leaves we can see how attached he is to Mickey and, by association, Mrs Johnstone. She realises the importance of the link between them
- Russell indicates that this isn't the end of the friendship when he relocates the Johnstone's to the country at the end of Act 1.

*Why the brothers grow apart and eventually die together in Act 2:*

- when Edward realises he too is in love with Linda and wants to marry her he is unaware that she is already married to Mickey and carrying his daughter/earlier sacrifices his own happiness to get Mickey to 'make a move'
- when Edward returns from his first term at university, we can see how the gap between his lifestyle and Mickey's has widened and deepened: each fails to understand the lifestyle of the other – Eddie fails to realise that his carefree 'bohemian' existence is so at odds with Mickey's unemployment and vice versa
- when Mickey slides into depression and is led into criminality (each exacerbating the other), he is unable to cope with life and becomes dependent on Valium/leaves Linda lonely for a life she's never had, pushing her into Eddie's arms
- the affair is the catalyst to the explosive end of the play. Mrs Lyons, in a clumsy/cruel attempt to sever Mickey's ties with Edward for good, tells Mickey about the affair
- Russell is careful, however, to make Mickey's anger 'boil over' at the point when Mrs Johnstone admits that the boys are brothers – he is angrier at his mother than his brother.

*Credit any relevant additional material. Use the relevant section of the Assessment Matrix on page 74 to score your essay.*

## Page 28: **Activity 3.12.1**

Friel: *Dancing at Lughnasa*

*Higher Tier* **Question about the family relationships**

The following textual details may be used to answer the question:

*What they say and do in the extract:*

- Agnes shows great concern for Rose: 'Oh God! Where could she –'/'What's happened to our Rosie?' – perhaps feels sense of responsibility for her going missing
- Kate wants to find out what happened and cross-examines Agnes with a series of questions/ urges her to get on with her explanation: 'Go on – go on!'

- Chris is practical in her approach: 'That means she's missing for over three hours'/'She wouldn't have gone into town in her Wellingtons'
- Kate angrily accuses Agnes of lying to her about Rose and Danny Bradley/withholding information with her: 'I've often seen you and Rose whispering together'/'You're lying to me, Agnes!' She demands to know the truth: 'I want to know everything you know! Now!'
- Maggie acts as peacemaker: 'That'll do Kate!' She takes control of the situation in a composed manner, suggesting possible explanations as to where Rose could be/calms situation down by being positive – 'She may be on her way home now'/'We're going to find her'/organises a search
- Kate objects to Maggie's suggestion to involve the police/she is concerned about generating gossip in the neighbourhood: 'I'm not going to have it broadcast all over'/'Mother of God, will we ever be able to lift our heads ever again ...?'
- Maggie's authority becomes evident at this moment of crisis when she interrupts Kate and tells her what is going to happen: 'I'm going to the police and you'll do what I told you to do'
- Agnes is gentle with Rose when she arrives home: helping her remember where the cans have been left/trying to protect her from Kate's reprimand: 'Later, Kate; after – '
- Maggie tries to divert attention away from Rose by changing the subject and discussing what they going are going to eat/joking about 'Eggs Ballybeg'
- Agnes, Maggie and Rose work together to get things back to normality: 'We'll go and pick some more bilberries next Sunday, Rosie'/'And you'd need to bring some turf in Rosie'/'How many pieces of toast do you want?'
- Chris tries to protect Rose from Kate's interrogation: 'Kate, just leave – '
- Kate intimidates Rose into telling the truth through persistent questioning
- Rose addresses her sisters, some individually, in a lengthy speech in which she defiantly states that she will say nothing more on the matter.

*Friel's use of stage directions and dramatic techniques in the extract:*

- they emphasise the sisters' feelings: *(Agnes begins to cry)*/Chris's impulse when she sees Rose – *(about to rush out to greet her)* but the wise Maggie *(catches her arm and restrains her)* so as not to make a fuss
- the detailed description of Rose/we 'see' through her sisters' eyes Rose's calm and natural behaviour as she approaches the house
- reveals Agnes's desire to hug Rose but she too restrains herself
- conveys Rose's nervousness as she evades the truth: *(Rose looks from one to the other)*/*(Rose has taken off her shoe and is examining it carefully)*
- helps convey the tension when Kate confronts Rose with her blunt demand: *(Rose moves towards the bedroom door)*/'I want to know where you have been, Rose'/*(Rose stops. Pause)*
- Rose's first attempt to tell the truth about where she'd been is described as *(inaudible)* which gives Kate the opportunity to demand that she speaks up
- the directions punctuating Rose's speech addressing her sisters are revealing
- Rose's dramatic exit which follows (*her shoes in one hand, the poppy in the other*).

*What the older Michael says about the sisters elsewhere in the play:*

- reveals how his Aunt Maggie – 'The joker of the family' – suggested the wireless should be called Lugh but Aunt Kate, 'a very proper woman' felt this would be sinful
- his reaction to the sisters' 'spontaneous step-dance'/he felt it was like voodoo, transforming his aunts into 'shrieking strangers'
- he was aware of the shame brought about by his mother having him out of wedlock/how the status of Uncle Jack's fame helped his aunt's reputation in the parish/his Aunt Kate's forebodings about Uncle Jack and Rose
- his satisfaction that his mother and father had a final dance together
- his insights into Maggie's behaviour after Rose and Agnes left
- his poignant account of the deaths of Rose and Agnes.

*Credit any relevant additional material. Use the relevant section of the Assessment Matrix on page 74 to score your essay.*

## Page 28: **Activity 3.12.2**

Friel: *Dancing at Lughnasa*

*Foundation Tier* **Question about Gerry**

The following textual details may be used to answer the question:

*What he says to Chris in the extract:*

- his evasiveness regarding how long its been since he last saw Chris and a present for Michael/always lets them both down/the bicycle never materialises – indicative of his well-meaning but empty promises: 'two dozen times I planned a visit and then something turned up'/'Actually I intended bringing him something small – '
- idiosyncrasies of speech which convey his effusiveness: 'Wow-wow-wow-wow'/'cross the old ticker'
- his unease is conveyed in his awkward pauses/lapses into cliché/over-zealous chatter: 'And how's Maggie?'/'Tell her I was asking for her – Agnes'
- his rose-tinted exaggeration about dancing lessons, being a gramophone salesman/we are unsure how much truth there is in them/caught out in a lie about gramophones but diverts Chris's attention by telling her to look at a magpie/irony of his words 'I'm a liar'/'Unbelievable'
- he can charm Chris and make her laugh/she joins in the banter about the cow
- tells her he is leaving for Spain 'With the International Brigade'/a little later in the conversation we learn he has 'still to enlist'
- admits his son is a stranger to him/makes no attempt to approach him.

*The reactions of the sisters to Gerry in the extract and elsewhere in the play:*

- Maggie has some sympathy for Gerry: 'looks terrified poor fella'/prepared to be welcoming: 'I'm sure he could do with a good meal'
- Kate's reaction in contrast: 'Terrified, my foot'/protective of Chris and very conscious of the damage he has already caused to the good name of the family and therefore she is unwelcoming: 'if she doesn't hunt him, I will'
- Agnes's persistent refusal to join her sisters in observing the encounter between Gerry and Chris/conveys her jealousy/she repeats 'Not just now' when invited to have a look/monosyllabic response and cynical reply when sisters discuss Chris and Gerry laughing together
- the evident contrast between how Maggie and Kate react to Gerry throughout the extract: Maggie reminds her that Gerry is Michael's father; Kate's response is a sarcastic, 'That's a responsibility never burdened Mr Evans'/Kate calls him a 'Tinker ... Loafer! Wastrel'
- the sisters' reactions to Chris and Gerry dancing: Kate calls Gerry 'The animal' and says 'He's leading her astray again'; Maggie says 'he's a wonderful dancer, isn't he?'; Agnes pretends she's too busy and says angrily 'For God's sake can't you see I'm busy!'
- Agnes's outburst at Kate calling Gerry, Mr Evans – this added to her earlier reactions suggests that she harbours her own special feelings for Gerry
- Kate's resentment about Gerry boils over: blames him for poisoning the atmosphere in the house/calls him 'the bastard'/concerned that 'Christina'll fall into one of her depressions'.

*Gerry's behaviour elsewhere in the play:*

- he asks Chris to marry him but she is realistic: 'Just dance me down the lane and then you'll leave'
- his antics while up the sycamore tree
- his dance with Agnes – Chris's jealousy very evident
- Michael reveals the contents of the letter he received from his half-brother, also called Michael, after Gerry's death informing him that his father was married/Michael's decision to shield his mother from this information.

*Credit any relevant additional material. Use the relevant section of the Assessment Matrix on page 74 to score your essay.*

## Page 29: **Activity 3.13.1**

Priestley: *An Inspector Calls*
*Higher Tier* **Question about Mr Birling**

The following textual details may be used to answer the question:

*Mr Birling's speech and behaviour in the extract:*

- he is condescending in his manner: 'You're new aren't you?'
- tries to impress: 'I was an alderman for years – and Lord Mayor two years ago–'
- his snobbery is conveyed in words such as: 'This is Gerald Croft – the son of Sir George Croft – you know Crofts Limited'
- his lack of concern for his workers is clearly evident: his refusal to raise their wages/called the strike a 'pitiful affair' and told the strike leaders 'Who'd started the trouble ... to clear out'/ 'If you don't come down sharply on some of these people, they'd soon be asking for the earth'
- his lack of sympathy for Eva Smith; he called her a 'wretched' girl
- he does not take any blame for what happened to Eva, even though he sacked her: 'Still, I can't accept any responsibility'
- he becomes increasingly aggressive as the Inspector keeps putting him on the defensive: 'I don't like that tone'
- tries to intimidate the Inspector by pointedly mentioning that the Chief Constable is 'an old friend'.

*How the Inspector reacts towards Mr Birling in the extract:*

- the Inspector doesn't allow himself to be manipulated by Mr Birling: refuses a drink of alcohol at the outset/doesn't give away any information
- Mr Birling tries to take control several times and sidetrack the Inspector: '– obviously it has nothing to do with the wretched girl's suicide. Eh Inspector?' but the Inspector remains undeterred: 'No, sir. I can't agree with you there'
- the Inspector refuses to be bullied/threatened by Mr Birling: 'But you asked me a question'/'It's my duty to ask questions'
- Mr Birling's attempts to impress the Inspector don't work: 'I don't play golf'.

*Priestley's use of stage directions in the extract:*

- show that Mr Birling is not in control of the situation – the Inspector is: (*He turns the desk chair a little away ... and sits*)/(*cutting through massively*)/(*He keeps his back to them*)
- they convey Mr Birling's increasing annoyance with the situation: (*with a touch of impatience*)/(*rather impatiently*)/(*turning to face the Inspector*)
- the details about the photograph reveal to the audience that Mr Birling knew Eva as he (*stares hard and with recognition*)
- they reveal that the Inspector is not taken in by Mr Birling: '(*drily*) I don't play golf'.

*Any other relevant examples from elsewhere in the play:*

- he states that 'a man has to mind his own business and look after his own' – mocks socialist ideas about community spirit and social responsibility
- Mr Birling's speeches during the engagement party come across as pompous and self-interested: 'We employees at last are coming together to see that our interests ... are properly protected'
- that he is self-opinionated: 'And I say there isn't a chance of war'/describes the Titanic as 'unsinkable, absolutely unsinkable'/'There'll be peace and prosperity' – Priestley wants audience to see Birling as arrogant and conceited
- his main concern throughout is to avoid a public scandal which would prevent him from getting his knighthood/sees this as his reward as 'a sound useful party man'/only interested in protecting his family's name rather than having any compassion for Eva Smith
- his son, Eric, revealingly states he was 'not the kind of father a chap could go to ... in trouble'
- he often gives orders and bosses his children about
- he's aggressive and sarcastic to Sheila at the end – becomes very self-assured when the Inspector is revealed to be a fake – until the phone call deflates his ego.

*Now use the relevant section of the Assessment Matrix on page 74 to score your essay.*



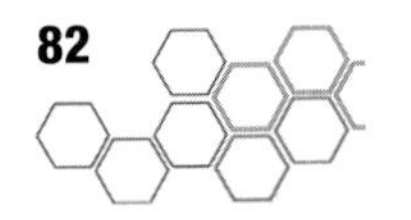

## Page 29: **Activity 3.10.8**

Priestley: *An Inspector Calls*
*Foundation Tier* **Question about Birling family life**

The following textual details may be used to answer the question:

*What the family say and how they behave in the extract:*

Mr Birling

- first thing he does is to round angrily on Eric: 'You're the one I blame for this'/he takes no responsibility for what happened: 'There's every excuse for what both your mother and I did –'
- his concern that 'There'll be a public scandal' and he 'was almost certain for a knighthood in the next honour's list' shows how full of his own importance he is
- he becomes *(rather excited)* at he thought that the Inspector might be a hoax and then angry at his family for allowing themselves to be 'bluffed' into confessing to the Inspector – only concerned about his public image
- shows no concern/compassion for Eva/dismisses her tragedy as 'nothing much has happened'/says they now must 'do something – and get to work quickly too' to avoid any scandal.

Sheila

- angry with her parents for their lack of concern: '*(scornfully)* That's all'
- takes responsibility for her own part: 'I behaved badly. I know I did, I'm ashamed of myself'
- she has learnt from her mistake and is upset that her parents 'don't seem to have learnt anything'.

Eric

- stands up to his father: 'what does it matter now whether they give you a knighthood or not?'
- he feels guilty about what he has done/he is ashamed of his behaviour and also that of his parents: 'But don't forget I'm ashamed of you as well – yes, both of you'
- (Sheila and Eric show more concern for others and are more sympathetic characters – Priestley seems to be saying that if society is going to change it will be through the efforts of the young.)

*Their attitude to the Inspector in the extract and elsewhere in the play:*

- Mr and Mrs Birling consider the Inspector 'rude' and impertinent/they have learnt nothing from what the Inspector has revealed of their roles in Eva's death
- it doesn't matter to Sheila if the Inspector was real. What is important to her is that the family learn to accept responsibility for the consequences of their actions/how their behaviour affects others
- Mr Birling is dismissive of the Inspector when he first meets him but becomes increasingly annoyed at his probing and questioning
- Mrs Birling is detached and comes across as cold and unfeeling when questioned about Eva Smith/she tries to put him in his place: 'You know of course that my husband was Lord Mayor only two years ago ...'

*How Eva Smith is treated elsewhere in the play:*

- Mr Birling sacked her for complaining about her wages/he refuses to take any responsibility for what happened as a consequence of this
- Mrs Birling refused to help the girl/it was only when she realises that the baby was her grandchild that she shows distress
- Mrs Birling shows no sympathy for Eva Smith: she called her death an 'absurd business'
- Sheila was self-absorbed at the start/she was 'very pleased with life and excited' about her engagement/did, however, show sympathy for Eva Smith, e.g. calls Mr Birling 'mean' for sacking her
- Sheila is open and honest about her involvement with Eva Smith/accepts her responsibility and expresses genuine sorrow when she finds out that her behaviour may have led to Eva losing her job
- Eric remembers little of the Eva episode as he was drunk/his behaviour was predatory and his relationship with her purely sexual/he described her as a 'good sport'

- Eric is also sympathetic towards Eva when he learns how his father sacked her
- Eric gets angry with his mother as he feels she killed his unborn child.

*Now use the relevant section of the relevant Assessment Matrix on page 74 to score your essay.*

# Chapter 4: The prose section

Assess your answer using the following individual checklists for each question, along with the relevant Assessment Matrix on page 74.

**In your essay there must be clear evidence that you have addressed the stem of the question.**

## Page 48: **Activity 4.11.1**

Johnston: *How Many Miles to Babylon?*
*Foundation Tier* **Question about the friendship between Jerry and Alexander**

The following textual details may be used to answer the question:

*The social and other differences between them:*

- Alexander is a privileged child from the 'big house'; Jerry is a 'peasant' boy, contemptuously referred to by Mrs Moore as a 'person from the village'
- cultural differences: Alex has a private piano tutor to teach him classical music; Jerry is more at home with the music of the blind fiddle player at the village crossroads
- they maintain their 'secret' friendship through meetings at the lake, during the dance at the village crossroads, or at their improvised 'riding school' on the hill behind the house
- their shared interests in horses and their dream of the future together, as owner and trainer of racehorses.

*How Alicia Moore and her husband tried to stop the friendship:*

- both his parents see his friendship with Jerry as an 'unsuitable relationship' and try in different ways to end it
- Alicia's firm ban on Alexander seeing Jerry 'I forbid it. Absolutely.' and the extended trip to Europe to separate them
- Alex's father tries a more gentle method, by encouraging him to take an interest in running the estate.

*The difficulties of maintaining their friendship in the army:*

- differences in rank – social contact between officers and men is discouraged
- Sergeant Barry's malicious attitude – he seems keen to get them into trouble with Major Glendinning
- they share some relief from the ugliness of trench life and further develop their friendship during the 'hunting' escapade or the trip to the French tavern
- they comfort each other in their sufferings: Jerry rubs brandy on Alexander's infected legs, Alexander gives Jerry his 'fleabag' when he returns from his supposed desertion
- Alexander appeals to Major Glendinning on Jerry's behalf, asking that he be allowed compassionate leave to search for his missing father
- the cruel way in which Major Glendinning tries to end their friendship – putting Alex in charge of the firing squad
- the shooting of Jerry as a final act of friendship?

*Now use the relevant section of the Assessment Matrix on page 74 to score your essay.*

## Page 48: **Activity 4.11.2**

Johnston: *How Many Miles to Babylon?*
*Higher Tier* **Question about Major Glendinning**

The following textual details may be used to answer the question:

*His harsh treatment of Alexander:*

- determination to teach Lieutenant Moore how to be a good officer, to 'make a man' of him
- dissatisfaction with Alexander's stand-offish behaviour and his refusal to 'mix' with the other officers



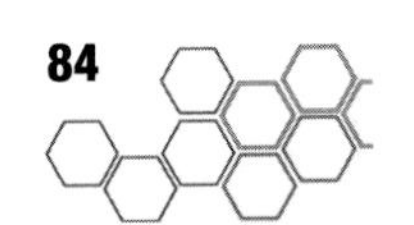

- strikes Alexander with his cane
- mockery of Alexander's weakness when helping him deal with the wounded soldier
- deliberate selection of Alexander as the commander of the firing squad which will execute Jerry: a cruel way of emphasising to Lieutenant Moore the necessity for 'impersonal' discipline in the army
- occasional glimpse of gentleness underneath: 'in the interests of humanity ... tell your men to shoot straight. It's over quicker if they do'.

*His strong sense of duty:*

- a hard-headed and experienced professional soldier, in contrast to the 'illiterate peasants, rascals and schoolboys' under his command
- pride in his military service, hence his violent reaction when he strikes Alexander for cynically referring to his uniform as 'some kind of fancy dress'
- suspicion of 'disaffection' in the Irish soldiers under his command: reference to Alexander's 'treacherous little country'
- feels he has no other choice than to treat his men like cattle
- at times feels the heavy burden of responsibility, having to make difficult decisions which endanger the lives of his men.

*The way in which he led his men:*

- contempt for the men under his command; refers to them as 'a bunch of damn bog Irish' and 'a sorry lot'
- his belief in 'strict impersonal discipline': there is no room in the army for 'emotionalists' like Alexander Moore and there must be no talking between the men and the officers
- lack of compassion for his men: refuses Jerry's request to be allowed to search for his missing father, accusing him of just wanting an 'easy billet'
- he is ruthless in the way he carries out his duty: warns that he will 'give no quarter' if there is indiscipline
- a harsh disciplinarian: 'severe punishments were meted out for the most trivial offences' and he has no scruples about imposing the 'ultimate' punishment, death
- he deals with the most difficult tasks personally: the patrol into no-man's-land to 'see to' the wounded soldier
- his men do follow him into battle; they do not have the same respect for Alexander or for Bennett.

*Anything else that is relevant may include:*

- the ambivalence of Alexander's feelings about the Major: 'I could never work out whether I hated or respected him'
- the symbolism in the constant polishing of his knife.

*Now use the relevant section of the Assessment Matrix on page 74 to score your essay.*

## Page 48: **Activity 4.12.1**

Orwell: *Animal Farm*

*Foundation Tier* **Question about Squealer**

The following textual details may be used to answer the question:

*How he changes the commandments:*

- devious ways in which he changes the commandments – the broken ladder and the overturned pot of paint
- exploits the fact that most of the animals do not have very good memories and therefore they cannot be sure what the original commandments were
- ongoing amendments to the commandments to excuse the increasingly privileged lifestyles of the pigs – 'No animal shall sleep in a bed – *with sheets*'!
- trains the sheep to chant the new slogan which allows the pigs to adopt the behaviour and the vices that characterised men: 'Four legs good, two legs better'.

*The sort of information he gives to the rest of the animals:*

- the use of statistics which appear to show that the animals are much better off now than under Jones
- his constant reminders that Jones could come back if the animals do not accept Napoleon's increasingly tyrannical rule
- use of lies to confuse the less intelligent lower animals and make them accept the privileges that the pigs take – the claim that it has been scientifically proven that milk and apples are absolutely necessary in the pigs' diet
- cruel pretence and hypocrisy in the account he gives of Boxer's death.

*How he defends Napoleon:*

- promotes the use of slogans and titles that glorify Napoleon: 'Napoleon is always right', 'Lord of the Sheepfold'
- identifies perceived enemies of Napoleon and marks them down for elimination in eventual purges
- ensures that any disasters on the farm (e.g. the fate of the first windmill) are put down to Snowball's malevolence rather than any incompetence on Napoleon's part.

*Anything else that is relevant might include:*

- his persuasive mannerisms – his excited style of talking, his 'shrill voice' and his 'twinkling eyes'
- he is a highly articulate and eloquent speaker who can 'turn black into white'
- he is often accompanied by the fierce farm dogs who ensure that his new rules are always accepted by the other animals.

*Now use the relevant section of the Assessment Matrix on page 74 to score your essay.*

## Page 49: **Activity 4.12.2**

Orwell: *Animal Farm*

*Higher Tier* **Question about the abuse of power**

The following textual details may be used to answer the question:

*The selfishness and greed of the pigs:*

- reserve the best food for themselves: the milk and apples
- laziness: they do no physical work themselves, merely direct the lower animals
- life of luxury: their occupation of the farmhouse
- their excesses: drunkenness
- education reserved for the young pigs and their 'secret police', the dogs
- eventually become 'indistinguishable' from men: their corruption is complete.

*The exploitation of the 'lower' animals, including Boxer:*

- use of constant hard labour (e.g. on the windmill) to ensure that the animals have no time or energy to plot revolts
- abolition of debates and elections so that the animals can have no voice in the development of the farm
- trade in animal products, such as the hens' eggs
- bloody purges to intimidate the lower animals into submission
- cruel exploitation of the faithful Boxer, in life ('I will work harder') and even in death (the case of whisky they were able to purchase through selling him to the knacker)
- insistence on the superiority of the pigs being recognised: other animals have to step aside when they meet a pig.

*Squealer's use of propaganda:*

- control of information: Squealer tells the animals only what he and Napoleon want them to hear
- the use of ridiculous statistics about economic production to persuade the animals that the farm is a success
- the focus on Snowball as the culprit when anything goes wrong on the farm, or as an excuse to eliminate any animal alleged to have associated with him
- the ongoing alterations to the Seven Commandments to accommodate the tyranny of Napoleon's rule



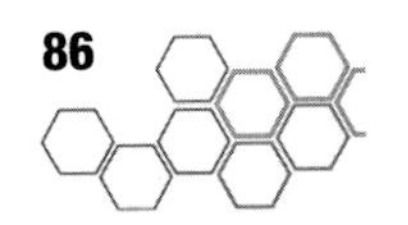

- the re-writing of history: new version of the roles of Snowball and Napoleon in the Battle of the Cowshed
- promotion of the cult of leader-worship: Napoleon as a god-like figure for the lower animals.

*Anything else that is relevant might include:*

- how Old Major's dream of freedom and equality for all is gradually corrupted
- how the gullibility of the lower animals is manipulated for the pigs' benefit
- how the corruption of the pigs is compounded by their stupidity: they are outwitted by humans in their haggling over the sale of the firewood
- how the tyranny of Napoleon's rule is reflected in the speeches at the final banquet in Chapter 10.

*Now use the relevant section of the Assessment Matrix on page 74 to score your essay.*

## Page 49: **Activity 4.13.1**

Lee: *To Kill a Mockingbird*

*Foundation Tier* **Question about Atticus as a parent**

The following textual details may be used to answer the question:

*What Jem and Scout think of their father:*

- before they learn to appreciate his other qualities, the children think he is not tough enough, compared to other fathers
- in the episode with the mad dog, Atticus shows he has the power to be a deadly marksman if he wishes, and the children are impressed
- they don't like to disappoint him or let him down. Jem's respect for his father is demonstrated when he returns to the Radley house to get his trousers, so that Atticus won't have to whip him.

*How he tries to teach them good behaviour:*

- he is prepared to let Jem face the justice system at the end of the novel
- he demonstrates personal bravery and the courage of his convictions when he stands up to the mob
- he insists that Jem apologise to Mrs Lafayette Dubose for cutting off the heads of her flowers
- Atticus invites Walter Cunningham to dinner and insists on Scout treating him with respect and acting as a good host
- Atticus forbids them to play the Radley game and stops them from putting a note through the letter box, thus emphasising the importance of a person's civil liberties.

*The example he sets them during his defence of Tom Robinson:*

- his honourable action in defending an innocent man, even though most members of the community are prejudiced against him and his action will have an adverse effect on his social life, business and personal credibility
- he stands up to his sister, Aunt Alexandra, and refuses to dismiss Calpurnia, despite the growing tensions in the town arising from his defence of Tom
- 'It's a sin to kill a mockingbird' – through his defence of Tom, he tries to teach his children the need to protect those that are more vulnerable
- 'You never really understand a person until you climb into his skin and walk around in it' – Atticus tries to teach the children to look at situations from another person's perspective
- his bravery – he stands up to the mob at Tom's cell
- he teaches his children to be understanding and tolerant of others, even those with prejudiced views – 'A mob's always made up of people, no matter what. Mr Cunningham was part of a mob last night, but he was still a man.'
- he lets the children hear the trial verdict.

*Anything else that is relevant might include:*

- Aunt doesn't approve of his parenting
- he is fair – he suspects that the children's game is to do with the Radleys, but they deny it and he has no proof, so he lets it go

- he doesn't preach to his children – he tries to guide them and let them work out situations for themselves.

*Now use the relevant section of the Assessment Matrix on page 74 to score your essay.*

## Page 49: **Activity 4.13.2**

Lee: *To Kill a Mockingbird*

*Higher Tier* **Question about Scout as a character we should admire**

The following textual details may be used to answer the question:

*Her relationship with her brother Jem:*

- they are very close and spend a lot of time playing games together, particularly at the start of the novel. She looks up to him
- distance between them grows as Jem matures more quickly, as the elder brother
- at the end of the novel he protects Scout from danger and ends up getting hurt. She shows concern for her brother.

*Her relationship with her father:*

- her father is her main role model – he sets her examples of civilised behaviour
- she has a very loving relationship with Atticus
- she doesn't enjoy school, where she is humiliated by Miss Caroline and punished. Atticus persuades her to return to school.

*Her involvement in some of the events of the story:*

- events are seen through her eyes, as she is the narrator of the novel. In her childish naiveté she does not fully understand the things she witnesses, therefore readers have to make sense of things themselves
- her involvement in the games at the Radleys' house
- key role in the defence of Tom Robinson – she is able to disperse the dangerous mob in a way which lightens a very tense situation. Through her naiveté and innocence she protects her father and Tom
- Calpurnia takes the children to her church where they face discrimination and resentment from Lula May
- her experiences during the pageant, when she and Jem set off on their 'longest journey together'. Symbolism here in that innocence is being attacked by evil.

*Anything else that is relevant might include:*

- the change we see in her throughout the novel – how her character is deepened and strengthened by her experiences
- despite being a tomboy for much of the novel, she eventually makes an effort to be more 'ladylike' – she attends missionary circle meetings and gives up fighting so much
- her understanding of Boo Radley.

*Now use the relevant section of the Assessment Matrix on page 74 to score your essay.*

## Page 50: **Activity 4.14.1**

Hill: *I'm the King of the Castle*

*Foundation Tier* **Question about Hooper as the villain of the story**

The following textual details may be used to answer the question:

*His bullying of Kingshaw:*

- Hooper makes Kingshaw feel unwelcome on his first arrival at Warings – the secret note which said 'I don't want you to come here'
- the first 'brief and wordless and violent scrap' between them on their first meeting
- Hooper's constant taunting of Kingshaw – e.g. about being a 'scaredy' or about his mother's lack of money
- the cruel trick of placing the stuffed crow on Kingshaw's bed
- Hooper exploits Kingshaw's fear of moths, trapping him in the Red Room
- Hooper torments Kingshaw by locking him in the dark shed
- threats about what will happen to Kingshaw when he joins Hooper at his school



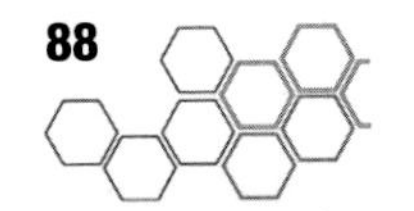

- Hooper destroys Kingshaw's one ray of happiness at Warings, his friendship with Fielding.

*How he lies to the adults:*

- as dysfunctional parents, both Mrs Kingshaw and Joseph Hopper easily accept Edmund's lies: Joseph Hooper admits that he is unable to 'assert' himself firmly with Edmund and Helena Kingshaw pays little attention to her son's protests about his cruel treatment by Edmund, as she is too concerned with the pursuit of her own happiness and security
- Hooper's allegation that Kingshaw had attacked him in Hang Wood causing him to fall into the stream and hit his head on the stone
- his allegation that Kingshaw had pushed him off the wall at Leydell Castle, breaking his leg
- Hooper's smug confidence that the adults will always accept his word.

*His own cowardice at times:*

- his terror of the thunderstorm in Hang Wood – 'he cried and blubbed – he peed with fright'
- his fear and terror when they are lost in Hang Wood, and his total dependence on Kingshaw to find a way out
- his intention to encourage his fellow bullies at school to torment Kingshaw
- his fear of heights at Leydell Castle.

*Anything else that is relevant might include:*

- the almost incredible naiveté of the adults: the problems between Kingshaw and Hooper are seen merely as: 'little upsets and frustrations, yes, little jealousies'
- Hooper's uncanny ability to follow Kingshaw everywhere, for example into Hang Wood – 'Hooper followed me. It's what he does'.

*Now use the relevant section of the Assessment Matrix on page 74 to score your essay.*

## Page 50: **Activity 4.14.2**

Hill: *I'm the King of the Castle*

*Higher Tier* **Question about the influence of setting on the behaviour of the characters**

The following textual details may be used to answer the question:

*Life for Kingshaw and Hooper at Warings:*

- oppressive atmosphere of the house: the 'solidity and gloom' of the place, with its 'heavy, sashed windows' and 'massive furniture'
- isolated and claustrophobic nature of Warings: Kingshaw feels trapped there, at Hooper's mercy
- it is a nightmarish place for Kingshaw: his fear and horror when trapped in the Red Room or in the shed
- the symbolism of Hooper's destruction of the Death's Head Hawk Moth
- Kingshaw finds no escape in the surrounding countryside: e.g. the attack on him by the crow, the eeriness of Hang Wood, his sense of repulsion at events on Fielding's farm
- two enemies, trapped together in the house, the boys malevolently destroy each other's models.

*Events in Hang Wood:*

- Kingshaw's journey to the Wood is shrouded in the dense morning mist
- the eerie sounds in the wood: 'some bird made a screeching sound, like a mad person laughing'
- the fungus growing on the decaying tree trunks, in 'weird, spongy shapes'
- the atmosphere in the wood becomes oppressively hot as the thunderstorm approaches
- the boys' imagined fears of what might be lurking in the wood: Kingshaw had 'a vision of things watching him'
- the violence of the storm – it tests the boys' reactions and exposes Hooper's weakness
- the expedition into the wood as a journey of self-discovery: Kingshaw's feeling that 'the wood had already changed him, enlarged his experience to a point where he was on the brink of discovering some secret'
- symbolism of the dead rabbit, with its 'maggotty wound'
- Kingshaw's resourcefulness: use of the ball of string in his efforts to try to find a way out of the wood.

*The trip to Leydell Castle:*

- Kingshaw feels a sense of freedom, of escape when he climbs the high walls of the castle: 'He felt high above them, very tall and strong and safe, too, nobody could touch him'
- his enjoyment of the climbing restores Kingshaw's confidence: he is nimble-footed and 'sure of his own judgement'
- the situation exposes again Hooper's weakness and enables Kingshaw to realise his superiority over Hooper: triumphantly he says, 'Up here, I'm the King'.

*Anything else that is relevant might include:*

- Kingshaw's occasional memories of situations in his previous school.

*Now use the relevant section of the Assessment Matrix on page 74 to score your essay.*

## Page 50: **Activity 4.15.1**

Steinbeck: *Of Mice and Men*

*Foundation Tier* **Question about types of violence in the novel**

The following textual details may be used to answer the question:

*The fight between Lennie and Curley:*

- George's earlier warning about the danger if Curley 'messes' with Lennie: 'Lennie ain't no fighter, but Lennie's strong and quick and Lennie don't know no rules'
- Curley's aggressive behaviour towards Lennie, from their first meeting: Lennie is a big man and, as always with bigger men, Curley sees him as a challenge
- Curley's vicious attack on Lennie, who refuses to defend himself until ordered by George to 'Get 'im.'
- Lennie almost effortlessly mangles Curley's hand, illustrating his frightening physical power
- Lennie's regret for his action afterwards: 'I didn't wanta hurt him'
- Curley's shame at the result of the fight: agrees to lie about the real cause of his injured hand.

*The killing of Curley's wife:*

- some sympathy generated for her, despite her aggressively flirtatious nature: 'I get lonely ... but I can't talk to nobody but Curley'
- ironically, just before her killing, she says Lennie is a 'kinda nice fella. Jus' like a big baby'
- she invites her own fate by making Lennie stroke her hair
- Lennie's panic and typical loss of self-control when she begins to scream
- horror in how easily he accidentally kills her: her body 'flopped like a fish' after he shook her
- Lennie' horrified, almost child-like reaction in the aftermath, as he realises he has 'done a real bad thing' this time.

*The shooting of Lennie:*

- the scene at the river as Lennie arrives: symbolism of the water-snake as the evil lurking in this apparent Garden of Eden
- George's decision to once again keep Lennie out of trouble, killing him quickly to protect him from the vengeance of Curley who is 'gonna shoot the guts outta that big bastard'
- tenderness of the final act of compassion: George repeats the familiar details of their shared dream just before he shoots Lennie
- the understanding shown by Slim who reassures George by saying, 'Never you mind. A guy got to sometimes'.

*Anything else that is relevant might include:*

- Lennie's history of unintentionally harming others: his 'assault' on the girl back in Weed
- the killing of the mouse and of the puppy
- the shooting of Candy's dog as a symbolic forerunner of Lennie's death.

*Now use the relevant section of the Assessment Matrix on page 74 to score your essay.*



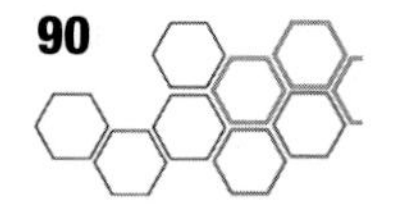

## Page 51: **Activity 4.15.2**

Steinbeck: *Of Mice and Men*

*Higher Tier* **Question about Lennie as a character we should feel sorry for**

The following textual details may be used to answer the question:

*His relationship with George:*

- Lennie is relatively helpless on his own: he cannot exist successfully without George's guidance and protection
- he sometimes suffers verbal abuse from George: George calls him a 'crazy bastard' and says 'If I was a relative of yours I'd shoot myself'
- George pays tribute to Lennie's loyalty and blind faith in him: 'he'd do any damned thing I told him'
- George's power over Lennie: he controls him by saying he won't allow him to look after the rabbits when they have their dream farm
- George's frustration with Lennie's simple-mindedness: 'He gets in trouble alla time because he's so God damn dumb'
- Lennie remembers and obeys George's instructions: he goes to the river at the end, as agreed with George
- the bond of trust and friendship between them illustrated by George's final act of compassion at the end.

*How he is treated by Curley and Curley's wife:*

- Curley sees Lennie as a challenge: on their first meeting he is at once 'calculating and pugnacious'
- Curley is determined to fight with Lennie, despite Lennie's obvious reluctance
- he is viciously violent towards Lennie, even when Lennie does not try to defend himself
- Curley is shamed and humiliated when Lennie crushes his hand
- his viciousness is illustrated at the end when he instructs Carlson to 'Shoot for his guts. That'll double 'im over.'
- Lennie notes that Curley's wife is 'purty' but he does not understand her 'games'
- George warns Lennie of the danger in Curley's wife: she is a 'piece of jail bait'
- Lennie unwittingly provokes Curley's wife by not responding to her attention-seeking, her 'ache for attention'
- she is attracted by Lennie's physical power, quickly realising that he had mangled Curley's hand, not a machine: 'OK Machine, I'll talk to you later. I like machines.'

*His 'dream':*

- he has no dream of his own. George allows him to share a part in his dream of their 'little place'
- Lennie's child-like nature is illustrated by his fascination with the rabbits: he would love stroking their soft fur
- his child-like innocence is also seen in the way he makes George tell him the story of their dream farm: 'It ain't the same if I tell it'.

*Anything else that is relevant might include:*

- the harshness of his life as an itinerant worker
- his instinctive feeling that the Tyler ranch is a 'mean' place. 'This ain't no good place. I wanna get outa here.'

*Now use the relevant section of the Assessment Matrix on page 74 to score your essay.*

## Page 51: **Activity 4.16.1**

Golding: *Lord of the Flies*
*Foundation Tier* **Question about Piggy as a wise and thoughtful character**

The following textual details may be used to answer the question:

*His concern for rules and organisation:*

- his respect for the conch as a symbol of order and civilisation
- tries to help Ralph control the meetings
- he has an adult sense of responsibility: he criticises the boys for behaving 'like a crowd of kids'
- his concern for the well-being of the 'littluns'
- sees the importance of practical things, such as building shelters, rather than indulging in the fun of hunting.

*How he tried to help Ralph be a good leader:*

- constantly reminds Ralph of the need to keep the signal fire going
- his attempts to persuade the boys that there is no 'beast' on the island – the only thing they have to fear is what is within themselves
- he tries to restore Ralph's morale after the shameful events of Simon's death
- his intelligent practicality – he suggests shifting the fire from the mountain to the beach
- symbolism of Piggy's glasses: he is the only one who can see reason and common-sense – the destruction of his glasses is the end of civilisation.

*How he tried to stand up against Jack and his savages:*

- his inability to convince the others of the good sense in his suggestions for surviving and being rescued
- his hatred of what Jack is doing to the boys – 'Which is better, law and rescue, or hunting and breaking things up?'
- his bravery and determination in deciding to face Jack and demand his glasses back
- the symbolism of Piggy's death: his last defence of civilised values, the shattering of the conch, the literal and metaphorical loss of his brains.

*Now use the relevant section of the Assessment Matrix on page 74 to score your essay.*

## Page 51: **Activity 4.16.2**

Golding: *Lord of the Flies*
*Higher Tier* **Question about leadership**

The following textual details may be used to answer the question:

*Ralph's sense of responsibility:*

- his essential good nature
- his belief in democracy and civilised behaviour – conduct of the assemblies
- his concern for the well-being of the 'littluns'
- personal bravery as a leader – going up the mountain to see if there is a 'beast'
- his frustration at the gradual desertions from his group
- his horror and guilt at his involvement in the ritual killing of Simon.

*Ralph's dependence on Piggy:*

- Piggy's constant advice – 'we should call an assembly'
- Ralph's inability to think clearly at times, his 'baffled common-sense' – he relies on his 'wise' friend Piggy to think things out for him
- Piggy's role as an embodiment of Ralph's conscience
- Ralph's isolation at the end, with no Piggy to help him.

*Jack's love of hunting and violence:*

- his dictatorial nature is seen at the outset, in his control of the choir
- his contempt for democracy – when he fails to unseat Ralph as leader, at a meeting, he takes his 'tribe' away, refusing to 'play' any more
- he undermines Ralph's sensible leadership – the boys see him as the provider of food, through his successful pig-hunts



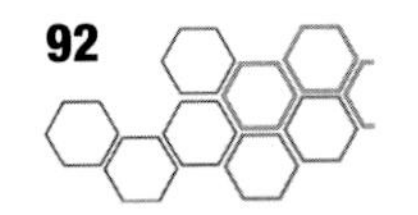

- Jack's irresponsible attitude – he would rather enjoy the fun of a pig-hunt than see to the practical necessities, such as keeping the signal fire alight
- his skill as a hunter turns into blood-lust
- Jack as bully – he takes his anger out on Piggy, rather than Ralph, striking him and breaking his glasses
- he leads the degeneration into savagery – chants and painted faces
- develops a cult of leader-worship – wants to be addressed as 'Chief'
- he rules his 'tribe' through violence and intimidation.

*Anything else that is relevant might include:*

- the sadistic Roger is Jack's henchman, as opposed to Ralph's good adviser, Piggy
- the final manhunt across the burning island.

*Now use the relevant section of the Assessment Matrix on page 74 to score your essay.*

# Chapter 5: *Poetry Anthology One*

## Page 54: **Activity 5.2**

1 Emphasising his regret; the wrongness of this action of felling these trees; and finally the repetition reinforces the fact that a number of trees was involved.

2 Each stanza opens with a succession of images that all suggest this cocooned, innocence that is so characteristic of childhood:

   i 'happy elf'
   ii 'tricksy Puck'
   iii 'cherub but of earth'
   iv 'pretty opening rose!'

3 This allows the poet to have his narrator, both consciously and unconsciously, begin to reveal his offensive, ruthless, egocentric nature. The manner in which this gradually unfolds has a shocking and cumulative effect upon the incredulous reader.

4 The natural images all suggest the extreme or transient nature of summer – for example, 'too hot the eye of heaven' or 'summer's lease has all too short a date' – and these contrast directly with the beauty of the young man that is 'more lovely and more temperate' now captured in the poet's 'eternal lines'.

5 The octet informs/instructs her love to remember her when she has gone 'into the silent land'. The sestet reveals the quality of her love and the nature of the remembering that she would like him to experience.

6 The reverse personification sees the wandering poet being compared to elements from nature, while the daffodils are viewed as displaying human qualities. This clever reversal alters our normal perspective and helps us to share Wordsworth's experience.

7 All his imagery is negative. They all combine to help build up the sense of bleakness that the poet is trying to create. We hear of 'spectre-gray' frost, 'tangle bine-stems' that 'score the sky' and 'strings of broken lyres'.

8 The imagery is simple and straightforward: 'rapid eyes' and 'like frightened beads'. This changes dramatically in the final six lines of the poem with the two stunning concluding extended metaphors that include 'Too silver for a seam', 'off banks of noon' and 'plashless'.

9 The archaic language has a simple and appropriately religious feel to it given that the poem is a prayer: 'Thy will be done' – a fragment from the Lord's Prayer – and 'but more O Lord, thine own'.

## Page 59: **Activity 5.3**

According to the Mark Scheme, candidates are most likely to select one of the following:

- 'My Last Duchess' by Robert Browning
- 'Upon My Son Samuel His Going for England, November 6, 1657' by Ann Bradstreet
- 'Remember' by Christina Rossetti

## Page 62: **Activity 5.4 and Activity 5.5**

**The scene or event which has affected each poet**

- Keats describes the richness of autumn.
- Shakespeare writes of the passing glory of summer.
- Hardy describes the severity of winter.

**General similarities and differences**

*The effect of the season on each poet:*

- Keats experiences fulfilment and peace for most of the poem
- Shakespeare contrasts his lasting love with transient summer
- Hardy is pessimistic and looks at nature as dead for most of the poem.

*How the poets use changes in tone or sustain their tone in these poems:*

- Keats and Hardy change their tone towards the end of their poems (Keats's pessimism or resignation surfaces and Hardy has found some grounds for optimism), whereas Shakespeare remains constant in his positive assertion that his love is more lovely than summer.

*The form of each poem:*

- 'To Autumn' - ode
- 'Shall I Compare Thee to a Summer's Day?' - sonnet
- 'The Darkling Thrush' - four eight-lined rhyming stanzas

*Who or what the poet is addressing:*

- Keats addresses autumn
- Shakespeare addresses his loved one
- Hardy's poem is reflective.

*Each poet presents a different attitude:*

- Keats openly expresses his admiration for the season through sensuous imagery
- Shakespeare expresses the beauty of his loved one made eternal through his lines, compared with the declining beauty of the glory of summer
- Hardy conveys how winter reflects his mood as a sympathetic background.

## Page 70: **Activity 5.8.1 and Activity 5.8.2**

Assess your answer using the following content-specific guidance, along with either the Higher or Foundation Tier Poetry Assessment Matrix on page 74.

**Examiners should note that candidates must address the stem of the question.**

Reward candidates who can:

- sensibly acknowledge and discuss similarities and differences
- offer an informed personal response
- back this up by a discussion of each poet's use of language.

*The place that has affected each poet:*

- Hopkins describes his real sense of loss
- Wordsworth describes how his spirits have been lifted by what he has seen
- Westminster Abbey reminds Beaumont of the transient nature of our existence.

**General similarities and differences**

*The effect of the place on each poet:*

- Hopkins experiences a sense of deep frustration at the thoughtlessness of those who felled these trees
- Wordsworth considers the ongoing pleasure that this sight still brings him
- The stark reminder that this is a fate none will escape offers a timely reminder to Beaumont.



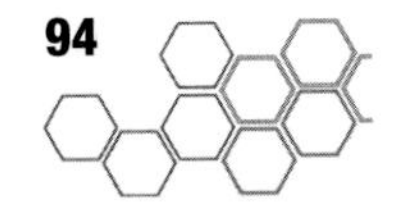

*Tone:*

Hopkins and Beaumont sustain their tone throughout their poems (Beaumont is stern and didactic, warning to his readers to take heed of his message, whilst Hopkins finds it difficult to understand the insensitivity of those responsible for this act of vandalism), and Wordsworth's joy at this wonderful sight is discovered to offer a second, reflective pleasure.

*The form of each poem:*

- 'Binsey Poplars' – two stanzas of eight and sixteen lines
- 'The Daffodils' – four six-line stanzas
- 'On the Tombs of Westminster Abbey' – rhyming couplets.

*Who or what the poet is addressing:*

- Hopkins appears initially to be addressing his felled trees and then the public at large
- Wordsworth poem is reflective
- Beaumont's addresses his readers.

*Each poet presents a different attitude:*

- Hopkins openly expresses his dismay and sense of loss through a painful central image; his imaginative use of language and his innovative sprung rhythm
- Wordsworth expresses his own sense of spiritual uplift upon initially seeing his daffodils through his use of inverted personification and the intimate, simple manner in which he is able to savour this pleasure by reflecting upon it afterwards
- Beaumont conveys his solemn message by including all the various social ranks of humanity as he points to the inevitability of the strikingly uncomfortable image 'flats the nose' and his final note 'to this shape all must be brought'.

**Similarities and differences in the poets' moods, and the candidate's personal preference**

Much of this will depend on the candidate's response to each poet's use of language. For example,

- versification and structure
- similes and metaphors
- alliteration and other 'sound' features
- visual imagery
- vocabulary choices
- repetition of words or ideas
- use of punctuation.

*Use the relevant Assessment Matrix on page 74 to score your essay.*

## Page 70-1: **Activity 5.9.1 and Activity 5.9.2**

**Question about love**

**Examiners should note that candidates must address the stem of the question.**

Reward candidates who can:

- sensibly acknowledge and discuss similarities and differences
- offer an informed personal response
- back this up by a discussion of each poet's use of language.

**Selection of a second poem**

This question is about love, how the poets convey the nature of this feeling, and the candidates' personal response. Candidates are most likely to select one of the following poems from this anthology to compare with 'Upon My Son Samuel His Going for England, November 6, 1657':

- 'Shall I Compare Thee to a Summer's Day?' by William Shakespeare
- 'Remember' by Christina Rossetti
- 'My Last Duchess' by Robert Browning
- 'A Parental Ode To My Son' by Thomas Hood

However, be receptive to other relevant selections, which are carefully argued.

**Textual details that may be used as supporting material**

'Upon My Son Samuel His Going for England, November 6, 1657' is about a mother's difficulties in reconciling the following:

- she loves her son and is anxious about the hazardous nature of his journey
- she is torn between her duty to God and her desire to see her son again safety returned
- her son was initially God's gift - an answer to her prayers and now she fears she may not survive to see him again
- finally she places herself in God's hands - 'Thy will be done'.

**Candidates' informed and personal response to the use of language**

Language analysis of 'Upon My Son Samuel his Going for England, November 6, 1657' may include some of the following features, which should be compared with the use of language in the other poem selected from the anthology:

- the mother's love for his son, shown in the intimate nature of her prayer to God ('The child I stay'd for many years')
- the powerful directness of deeply felt, if restrained, emotion ('son of prayers, of vows, of tears')
- the simplicity of the mother's appeal to God ('Thy will be done')
- the sense of a mother struggling to keep her emotions in check ('He's mine, but more, O Lord' thine own')
- the use of first person adding to the very personal feel of the prayer ('I here resign into thy hand')
- her final peace-making with her God ('persuade my heart ...')
- the unusual and positive verb used in the final line ('happefy'd').

How the speaker in the other selected poem conveys love will depend upon the choice - there is a range of potential options. **Reward candidates whose consideration derives from an informed, personal response to the poet's stance and use of language.**

*Now use the relevant section of the Assessment Matrix on page 74 to score your essay.*

## Page 71: **Activity 5.10.1 and Activity 5.10.2**

**Question about unexpected encounters**

**Examiners should note that candidates must address the stem of the question.**

Reward candidates who can:

- sensibly acknowledge and discuss similarities and differences
- offer an informed personal response
- back this up by a discussion of each poet's use of language.

**General similarities and differences**

*The effect of the encounter on each poet:*

- Dickinson is at first amused by her meeting with the bird before finally being impressed by the bird's flight
- Wordsworth considers the ongoing pleasure that this sight still brings him
- Hardy is struck by the divergence between his mood and that of the joyful thrush.

*Tone:*

Wordsworth sustains his positive tone throughout the poem whereas Dickinson and Hardy both change the tone of their poems as a result of their encounters (Dickinson is, initially, quite patronising in her tone but this changes to awe when she recognises the awesome beauty of its flight and Hardy's darkly pessimistic mood is lifted by his encounter with the thrush).

*The form of each poem:*

- 'A Bird Came Down the Walk' - five quatrains
- 'The Daffodils' - four six-line stanzas
- 'The Darkling Thrush' - four octets.



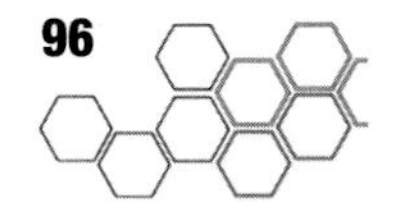

*Who or what the poet is addressing:*

- Dickinson is almost conversationally describing her encounter for the reader
- Wordsworth poem is reflective
- Hardy shares his experience with his readers.

*Each poet presents a different attitude:*

- Dickinson openly expresses her amusement at the bird's behaviour, before expressing her compassion for the creature in her ill-considered by vain attempt to feed it prior to the series of luxurious images that capture the magical quality of its flight as it escapes her unwelcome attentions
- Wordsworth expresses his own sense of spiritual uplift upon initially seeing his daffodils. This is developed through his use of inverted personification and the intimate, simple manner in which he is able, afterwards, to savour this pleasure by reflecting upon it
- the oppressively bleak nature of his surroundings seems to be weighing heavily upon Hardy until a thrush bursts into song. Such is the joy that imbues the song that the poet begins to wonder if this small creature knows something of which he is 'unaware'.

**Similarities and differences in the poets' moods, and the candidate's personal preference**

Much of this will depend on the candidate's response to each poet's use of language.
For example:

- versification and structure
- similes and metaphors
- alliteration and other 'sound' features
- visual imagery
- vocabulary choices
- repetition of words or ideas
- use of punctuation.

*Now use the relevant section of the Assessment Matrix on page 74 to score your essay.*

## Page 72: **Activity 5.11.1 and Activity 5.11.2**

**Examiners should note that candidates must address the stem of the question.**

Reward candidates who can:

- sensibly acknowledge and discuss similarities and differences
- offer an informed personal response
- back this up by a discussion of each poet's use of language.

**Selection of a second poem**

This question is about sorrow and loss, how the poets convey the nature of this feeling, and the candidates' personal response.

Candidates are most likely to select one of the following poems from this anthology to compare with 'Remember':

- 'Break, Break, Break' by Alfred Lord Tennyson
- 'Remembrance' by Emily Brontë
- 'Binsey Poplars' by Gerard Manley Hopkins.

However, be receptive to other relevant selections, which are carefully argued.

**Textual details that may be used as supporting material**

'Remember' is about the narrator's death and the effect of that parting upon the lover left behind. It is about a lover's struggle (most probably the poet herself, given the intimate nature of the work, allied to the fact that she wrote it when she was nineteen and engaged to be married) to come to terms with the following:

- the pain of separation from her love

- her desire to be remembered but not to cause her love further grief
- her ultimate wish for her lover that he be happy.

**Informed and personal response to the use of language**

Language analysis of 'Remember' may include some of the following features, which should be compared with the use of language in the other poem selected from the anthology:

- the intimate nature of the subject matter is reflected in the first person narration and the frequent use of 'I' and 'you'
- the intimate nature of their present relationship ('When you can no more hold me by the hand'/'tell me of our future that you planned')
- the powerful poignancy of the early images ('I half turn to go yet turning stay')
- the euphemisms for death ('the silent land'/'darkness and corruption')
- the manner in which the sonnet form is used to carry/develop the poem's ultimate message
- the building up of the evocation to 'remember' that builds through the poem
- the simplicity of the final two lines capture the selfless quality that is at the heart of real love.

How the speaker in the other selected poem conveys his/her sense of sorrow and loss will depend upon the choice – there is a range of options. **Reward candidates whose consideration derives from an informed, personal response to the poet's stance and use of language.**

*Now use the relevant section of the Assessment Matrix on page 74 to score your essay.*